MASTER *your* FUTURE

The Roadmap for the Rest of Your Life

AGINGOPTIONS
Educate • Train • Connect

Author

Rajiv Nagaich, J.D., LL.M.

Editor

Gayla Zoz

Creative Services

Gwen Canfield

Contributors

Bob Pittman

Carol Redfield

AGINGOPTIONS

Educate • Train • Connect

www.AgingOptions.com

Master Your Future

Welcome to Master Your Future Workbook!

I'm delighted that you are taking this opportunity to create a better plan for your retirement in a way that supports your local public television station.

Creating your LifePlan for retirement will be an exciting journey of self-discovery, one to savor and enjoy. As you go through the process in this workbook, questions may arise. I invite you to explore the many resources at AgingOptions.com. You will find the answers there.

AgeOn!

Rajiv Nagaich, J.D., LL.M., NAELA Fellow
Author of Master Your Future Workbook

Second Edition

Published by Bright Images, Inc.
brightimagesmedia.com
sales@brightimagesmedia.com

BRIGHTIMAGES

Printed in the United States of America

ISBN 978-0-9994573-9-9

Master Your Future

Introduction

When you hear the word 'Retirement' what images come to your mind? Relaxation? Time for reflection? Time to pursue new interests? Time with loved ones? Our thoughts are generally positive, pretty simple, and with a measure of excitement.

As we reach our golden years, perhaps we think of it as a time of long-awaited celebration with no worries. But wait! Have we considered any obstacles, any special needs, any unforeseen crises? Have we totally prepared ourselves and our family for the meaningful journey ahead?

The purpose of this book is not to instill fear or anxiety in our participants. Quite the contrary! We want to add to your confidence and assurance that you have taken the proper steps to embrace these golden years knowing that you:

1. **Avoid institutional care** by developing a framework of calculated directives
2. **Avoid running out of money** by protecting assets from uncovered medical and long-term care costs
3. **Avoid becoming a burden on loved ones** by establishing communication and empowerment with your family/loved ones.

These objectives stem from the most common concerns for retirees, and they illustrate the uncertainty surrounding a typical approach to retirement and the all-too-common results. And these concerns aren't without merit, because inadequate planning falls short of achieving these objectives for many Americans. Hereafter, we'll refer to the typical retirement planning done by most seniors as "**Traditional Planning.**"

Welcome to LifePlanning™ with Aging Options

In the following pages, we will help you navigate the five essential pillars of retirement: Health, Housing, Financial, Legal, and Family, pulling them all together into one comprehensive *LifePlan™*.

We'll ask you to answer a number of questions, which will evoke deeper discoveries and guide you along to make important decisions. Then, with additional guidance and support, you will develop your own personal Blueprint to enable you to cultivate the future you desire and to maintain your quality of life.

You have taken the first important step to achieving these comforting results. With a retirement plan that is comprehensive and more secure than traditional planning can ever be, you will soon realize that there is more to it than merely completing your bucket list.

Traditional planning is fragmented and rarely considers the three-fold objectives, instead focusing on individual segments of planning…and that can lead to disaster.

By the end of the book, you will have your own personal plan—created by YOU! Not to mention a new-found, gratifying peace of mind.

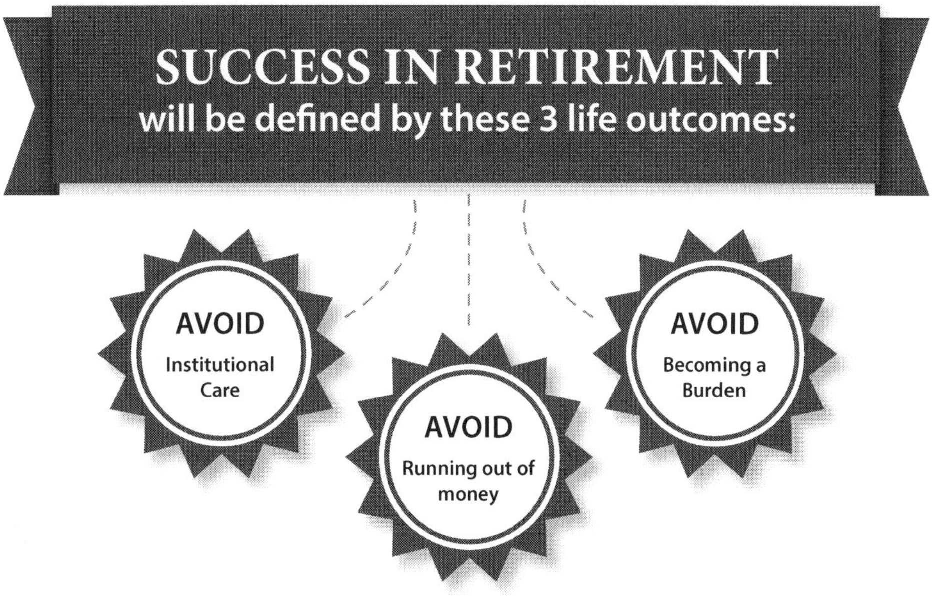

"Traditional Planning" vs *LifePlanning*

To appreciate LifePlanning, we need to take a look at the way most Americans approach retirement and identify the problems that arise.

The Domino Effect of Traditional Retirement Planning

Unfortunately, traditional retirement planning can often be disastrous because the elements of a typical plan are fragmented and conflicting. Pretend for a minute that you are a retiree with a traditional retirement plan. More than likely you have enrolled in Medicare. You have paid off your home and are hoping to age there until a time you no longer can, and you will move when the time comes. Thanks to your financial planner you also have a sizable nest egg to last the rest of your life. You have seen an attorney and created a Trust, Will, Powers of Attorney, and a Living Will or an Advance Directive. Are you prepared for retirement? Maybe, maybe not. For a small few, traditional planning is enough. For most, it is nothing short of a disaster.

Imagine yourself sitting at home one day—successfully retired—watching your favorite TV show. In the middle of the show, without warning, you experience a massive headache. Something in the pit of your stomach tells you that this is not an ordinary headache. You dial 911. The EMTs crash through the door, start attending to you, realize you are suffering a stroke, and rush you to the closest hospital.

This episode starts out being a health issue. After initial treatment, the attending physician advises you to exercise, socialize, change your diet, and lose some weight. Then the physician signs the discharge papers that send you to a rehabilitation center to receive physical, speech, and occupational therapy. You are given a list of centers to choose from and, because you never considered the possibility that you would have to choose a rehabilitation center, you have no knowledge upon which to base your decision. The hospital chooses the rehabilitation center (usually housed in a nursing home) for you. You have no idea as to the quality of the rehabilitation center chosen for you. Nor do you know when you will be handed your discharge papers.

You, like most Americans, never wanted to see the inside of a nursing home from a patient's perspective. However, since this nursing home stay is supposedly part of the healing process, you accept it—for now! You hope to make a rapid recovery and return home soon. For the first two or three weeks, you throw yourself into the process, hoping that if you stick with the rehabilitation program, you will soon be home. But as time passes by, people keep telling you that you aren't healthy enough to return home. When your spouse or child visits wanting to know how you are feeling, all you can think to ask them is, "When am I getting out of here?" You don't want to admit it, but your health situation has made living at your home the way you were unattainable. You and your family now have a housing issue to deal with. You want to go home but everyone around you insists that this isn't possible at the current time. Still, you refuse to panic because no matter how tired you are of being in the nursing home, at least Medicare is covering the bill.

You expect Medicare to cover the bill for 100 days because the booklet from the Department of Health and Human Services on Medicare Coverage says on page 14 that you can get up to 100 days of Skilled Nursing Facility (nursing home) coverage.

So you, being unaware that "up to" means that the number can be significantly smaller than 100 days, are surprised when, on day 22, a social worker walks into your room on a Friday and informs you that you have stopped making progress. And for that reason, Medicare is going to stop paying for your care on Monday. You now have one weekend to make other arrangements. What are your options? Home? This is only an option if your home has become equipped for you to safely stay in, which, depending on your financial, family, and health situation is probably unlikely.

What are your other options? You can remain in the nursing home and pay privately. But what will that cost? It depends. For instance, if you desire to continue to rehabilitate, the cost will likely average between $15,000 to $18,000 per month. But, if you choose to give up trying to rehabilitate and only desire to access long-term care services in a less clinical setting, such as an assisted living facility, the cost will be a bit more reasonable—a Seattle-area average is between $9,000 to $12,000 per month.

Medicare will not cover any of these costs in any meaningful way. If you don't have a good long-term care insurance policy to help you with these costs, your stroke (which was first a **health issue**, then a **housing issue**) has now become a **financial issue**.

If you are lucky, someone will advise you to see an Elder Law Attorney. You may ask, "Why do I need to see a lawyer when I have my legal affairs in order?" You have a Will or Trust, Powers of Attorney, and a Living Will—all the documents you were advised that you would ever need to have in order to retire.

The answer is that an Elder Law Attorney can help you obtain funding to cover the exorbitant long-term care costs you now must cope with. And, if you find the right Elder Law Attorney, that attorney will help coordinate the planning with the medical and housing professionals, so you don't find yourself bouncing from one facility to another before you finally find your permanent placement. So, despite having all your legal affairs in order, you find that your health issue morphed first into a housing issue, then a financial issue, and has now become a **legal issue**.

And your family, meanwhile, has been doing everything they can to help you, but they have no idea how to even start coordinating your care, paying your bills, or whom to contact for information. If you have not planned well and defined your wishes, your family must guess what you want at each step in the process, whether that was your intention or not. This is why, at the end of the day, your retirement is truly a **family affair**.

You can see how one illness can turn seemingly disconnected aspects of life into one connected episode. Unless you have a comprehensive and well-coordinated retirement plan that addresses all five of these disciplines, you will find that your traditional planning is costing you financially, restricting your decisions, and rendering you an undue burden on others.

Luckily, YOU are beginning your LifePlanning journey to help you achieve a better outcome.

How to use this Workbook

LifePlanning is divided into sections based on the key aspects of life that require planning and coordination but are so often planned separately from each other in the traditional style of retirement planning. The essential aspects are Health, Housing, Financial, Legal, and Family... and together they form what we call "The Five Pillars" of a comprehensive *LifePlan*.

We encourage you to follow the planning process in the order presented in this program. Since the emphasis is on Housing, start your work there. Next, proceed through Health, Financial, Legal, and then end with Family. We also recommend that you follow the content contained in each chapter in the order that the information is presented. *LifePlanning* builds upon previous concepts and information, so it will be more meaningful if you follow it in order.

By the end of each chapter, you should narrow down your decisions and preferences. If you are following the program as outlined, you will have gained insight into what professional services you need to work with. Using the worksheets provided, record your decisions along the way, highlight focus areas, and cross off irrelevant ones. By the end, you'll have your personalized *LifePlan* Blueprint! This will give you a clear idea about your precise goals, and how to go about fulfilling them.

Once you have completed each chapter, transfer your answers from the worksheets to your convenient *LifePlanning* Blueprint in the last chapter of this workbook. This will help you have all your decisions easily accessible when you meet with your family and professionals.

Implementing Your *LifePlan*

Remember, this is just the planning process...

After you've created your *LifePlan* Blueprint, now comes the work of implementing it. We recommend prioritizing each decision you have made and work on only one planning aspect at a time (Housing, Health, Financial or Legal) so that implementing the *LifePlan* does not become an overwhelming experience. Deploying your *LifePlan* does not need to follow the same order of events as your Blueprint; you can implement your decisions in any order you choose.

Resources

One last thing... Take advantage of our extensive network of experienced and dedicated professionals who are ready to assist you in these life-shaping decisions. You can find them in our Resource Guide, referenced throughout this program. These professional resources are provided for your convenience to help you complete your *LifePlan*.

Are you ready to get started? Let's dive in!

Take advantage of extra help in...

The Portal

Congratulations! You've taken the first step toward creating your own *LifePlan*. It's the best way to lay the groundwork for successful retirement, one where you avoid institutional care, avoid becoming a burden on loved ones, and have money left at the end.

QUICK SUCCESS TIP: Your workbook grants you a free trial of ***The Portal***, which gives you access to **AgingOptions Academy**. That's where you'll find the *LifePlanning* Retirement Planning Program, an online course containing videos, checklists, reading material, assessments, and other information that will serve as an excellent online companion as you go through your workbook.

Take advantage of everything your free trial of ***The Portal*** has to offer!

Access your free trial of ***The Portal*** at:

Resources.AgingOptions.com

AgingOptions LifePlanning™

Health Planning

For Your Retirement

How to Plan for Your Healthcare Needs

Healthy people do not end up in institutional care settings, become a burden on loved ones, or lose assets to uncovered care costs, so your continued good health is your most important asset in retirement. Do everything you can to protect it.

They say the greatest wealth is health. And, as we move through our retirement years the quality of our health will have an enormous impact on the quality of our lives.

One illness can pull together seemingly disconnected aspects of life into one difficult episode that throws all of your plans into disarray.

LifePlanning offers a well-coordinated and comprehensive approach to retirement planning to help you avoid the usual pitfalls and financial costs of traditional planning by bringing together essential disciplines, making sure your wishes are specific and clear, and letting loved ones know the details and their specific role in your plans. Through this process, you will be able to anticipate and navigate whatever retirement challenges arise.

While we all look to our insurance plans and one of the most advanced healthcare systems in the world to help us in the event of illness or disability, perhaps we should be looking to those same services to help us stay healthier along the way.

In the Health pillar of *LifePlanning* by AgingOptions, we help you understand how you can be proactive about your Health and how it is connected to the rest of your life.

Your Health is your greatest asset. We cannot stress strongly enough that success in retirement means you accomplish these three goals:

- **Avoid institutional care**
- **Avoid running out of money due to uncovered medical and long-term care costs**
- **Avoid becoming a burden on loved ones**

Do you want to know the secret to accomplishing these goals?

Don't become ill!

No, that's not a joke. Think about it…the longer you stay healthy, the longer you can avoid the retirement nightmares the majority of retirees end up facing.

But, don't count on traditional healthcare planning for much help with this issue. Traditional planning around healthcare needs in retirement begins with enrolling in Medicare and buying a supplemental insurance plan expecting the insurance policy to cover all healthcare-related expenses.

The mainstream approach to health is on helping you gain access to medical care *after* you fall ill. Precious little is done to help you not fall ill. That is the hole you have to fill if you desire not to end up in institutional care against your wishes.

The primary focus of a good healthcare plan *should* be to help you prolong your healthy years and avoid becoming ill in the first place. An important, but secondary, focus is knowing how to deal with an illness if, despite your best efforts, you do end up falling ill.

Of course, if you do become ill, America is a great place for that to happen. It has cutting-edge solutions to stitch, patch, and dose you back to health, especially if you know where to look.

What Is Wrong with Our Healthcare System?

Healthcare in the United States has both strengths and weaknesses when it comes to our overall well-being. The most glaring weakness is that our system doesn't place a high enough value on staying healthy.

Despite spending the most amount of money on healthcare than anywhere else in the world[1]—about $10,000 per person each year—Americans do not have the longest lifespans[2], nor do we have the healthiest lifespans[3]. That is what is wrong with our system.

1 Henry J Kaiser Family Foundation. (2011). Snapshots: Health care spending in the United States & selected OECD countries. Retrieved from www.kff.org/health-costs/issue-brief/snapshots-health-care-spending-in-the-united-states-selected-oecd-countries/

2 Life expectancy at birth (years), 2000-2016: Both sexes: 2016. Retrieved from gamapserver.who.int/gho/interactive_charts/mbd/life_expectancy/atlas.html

3 The Commonwealth Fund. (2014). Mirror, mirror on the wall, 2014 update: How the U.S health care system compares internationally. Retrieved from https://www.commonwealthfund.org/publications/fund-reports/2014/jun/mirror-mirror-wall-2014-update-how-us-health-care-system

How did the system get that way? Consider the following:

- Who in the healthcare system will make money when you are not ill?
- Which hospital will be profitable when you do not use hospital services?
- Which pharmaceutical manufacturer will make money when you do not buy pills?
- Which medical practice will make money when you do not show up at the clinic?

The information you need to prolong your healthy years and postpone falling ill is available. But if the healthcare industry does not make money, it is unlikely you will get that informatoin from the industry. It will be up to you to educate yourself on how to use the healthcare system so you can prolong your healthy years.

We will show you how you can actually change the way you use the traditional medical system to shift the emphasis from access to care after you fall ill to using the same system to not fall ill in the first place.

Healthy Habits

What is the prescription to not fall ill?

Develop Healthy Habits

- **Eat right**
- **Exercise**
- **Socialize**

Surely, this isn't new information to anyone. But why is it so difficult for us to do? Is there any help we can get to improve our habits?... Let's answer these questions by looking at these key healthy habits individually.

Eat right

Eating right means eating healthy and making healthy choices with your food. There are many trendy fads in the world of dieting and clean eating, but there are a few that are consistently recommended and evidence-based. They include eating lots of fruits and vegetables, consuming the necessary amount of nutrients (such as the correct ratio of protein-rich foods proportionate to your weight), decreasing caloric intake, and paying attention to portion sizes.

Eating healthy has been proven to reduce chemicals associated with inflammation, improve sleep and mood, boost energy levels, improve memory, and lower the risk of Alzheimer's disease.

One of the simplest tools that is available to you in your traditional healthcare system is a consultation with a nutritionist. If proper diet can help keep high blood pressure, high cholesterol and the chronic ailments away, why would a nutritionist not be as important, if not more so, than a primary care provider who will diagnose the ailment only after some damage has been done?

Although today, Americans enjoy longer lifespans compared to past generations, they also live some of their additional years with

increased disabilities. One major cause is the poor American diet. It isn't only bad eating habits that plague the American diet but a lack of information as well.

Recent developments in nutrition studies suggest that what many of us were taught even twenty-five years ago was largely incorrect (just look at a food pyramid from the 1990s where it recommends eating six to eleven servings of bread and pasta a day). This illustrates why a nutritionist is so important. Not only do they encourage good eating habits, but they also clear up misconceptions using the latest nutritional science and research.

Although nutritionists are valuable assets when it comes to your health, not all insurance carriers cover the services of nutritionists. Call your insurance company to see if your insurance covers a nutritional consultation. If not, consider opting into a program that does. Take a look at your own eating habits.

These habits include:

- **Eating lots of fruits and vegetables**
- **Eating the needed amount of nutrients (such as the correct ratio of protein-rich foods proportionate to your weight)**
- **Decreasing caloric intake**
- **Paying attention to portion sizes**

It is important to take an honest look at what you eat and how much, then make decisions on how you can improve. Let's define how we rate eating habits:

Excellent: You have excellent eating habits if you identify with ***ALL*** of the following:

- ☐ You pay close attention to creating varied, well-balanced meals.
- ☐ You eat the right portion sizes for your physical requirements, age, and size.
- ☐ You strictly follow personalized dietary instructions from your medical team for any existing health concerns.

Fair: Your diet is considered Fair if your habits fall ***MOSTLY*** in this category:

- ☐ You eat a varied diet but you don't deliberately strive for balanced meals.
- ☐ You eat reasonable portion sizes but you don't monitor caloric intake.
- ☐ You try to limit foods you know aren't good for you but you cheat sometimes.

Poor: Your diet would qualify as poor if you identify with ***ANY*** of these statements:

- ☐ You rarely monitor the foods you eat to maintain a balanced diet.
- ☐ You don't moderate the amount of food you consume.
- ☐ Your diet consists mainly of processed foods or fast food.
- ☐ Your weight is a concern because of your diet.
- ☐ You ignore dietary recommendations from your doctor about things that are contributing to a health condition (such as gastrointestinal problems, allergies, diabetes, etc.).

Where there is room for improvement, make plans to move up a level from where you are currently. Set a goal to make this improvement this month.

How are you doing with your eating habits lately? Select the options that most reflect your habits and make notes about what you'd like to focus on regarding this topic.

Healthy Lifestyle: Eat Right

My current eating habits are: (Select one)

- ☐ Excellent
- ☐ Fair
- ☐ Poor

I would like to meet with a nutritionist:

- ☐ Yes
- ☐ No
- ☐ Undecided

Notes regarding my Healthy Eating Plan:

Exercise

Regular exercise benefits everyone regardless of age, and can even help to improve the lives of people with chronic health problems. Some of the benefits include:

- Improves energy and self-confidence
- Lessens anxiety and depression
- Contributes to a healthy body weight, which in turn relieves weight-bearing joints, improves blood pressure, and lowers blood sugar and blood fat levels
- Helps prevent blood clots, which is a particular benefit to people with heart- or blood-related diseases
- Improves sleep, which plays a critical role in immune function, and is one of the strongest anti-inflammatory tools we have to help reduce disease
- Strengthens muscles, which will help to improve gait and balance, and reduce the risk of falling
- Leads to greater intellectual vigor, specifically improvements in executive function. This is important because executive function, which is responsible for emotional and cognitive control, tends to fade as we age.

And the list goes on!

With all of these benefits, it only makes sense to include exercise as part of your retirement plan.

Take an honest look at your activity level, then make decisions on how you can improve. Let's define how we rate physical activity:

- **Physically Fit:** You make it your business to get your heart rate up, sweat, and proactively pursue physical fitness consistently.
- **Active:** You regularly move around the house or the yard, but you rarely engage in vigorous activity on any consistent basis.
- **Sedentary:** You don't move much. You may get around the house, but not much more.

Since exercise plays such a large role in helping you prolong your healthy years, whatever level you are currently, we suggest that you aim to move up a level over the next three months.

Here are some goal suggestions:

- **If you identify as Physically Fit**, good for you! Keep up the good work and continue to monitor your activity level and make adjustments as you age to keep yourself healthy, safe, and active.
- **If you identify as Active**, your goal should be adding a routine to get your heart rate up and perspire a bit. If you find that to be difficult, see if your health insurance policy includes gym privileges; if not, look for a policy that does during the next open enrollment and then use those benefits to create a healthier future. Going to a gym will allow you the opportunity to work with a personal trainer. Research shows that when you make yourself accountable to someone for personal behavior, you will be more likely to follow through on your commitments.
- **If you identify as Sedentary**, among the simplest ways to become active is to start walking more. Try a goal to work your way up to walking 10,000 steps a day, if possible, using a wearable device that measures your steps. If your physical condition is such that you cannot walk, consider water exercises. These can be found at many community centers or fitness facilities. See the comments above regarding insurance policies.

**Be sure to consult your physician about what exercises would be appropriate for you.*

Remember, the longer you are healthy, the longer you will stay away from institutional care settings, avoid becoming a burden on loved ones, and avoid burning through your life savings to pay for uncovered long-term care costs.

Now, take a moment to think about your own exercise regimen and answer the following questions:

Healthy Lifestyle: Exercise

My current physical activity level is: (Select one)

- ☐ Physically Fit
- ☐ Active
- ☐ Sedentary

My plan to improve my exercise includes: (Select all that apply)

- ☐ Joining a gym or other active group
- ☐ Checking if my insurance will cover gym memberships
- ☐ Monitoring my steps (via phone app or wearable device)
- ☐ Other

Notes regarding my exercise plan: (See goal suggestions)

Socialize

Taking steps to establish and maintain a healthy lifestyle will help to preserve and protect our retirement goals. An important component of a healthy lifestyle is socializing. There are now some compelling statistics to help encourage plenty of culture and community.

As we age, the effect of social isolation and loneliness increases, and this is experienced by as many as forty percent of aging adults. Why is this such a problem? Research indicates that loneliness often equals depression and accelerates cognitive decline (our ability to remember). Sadly, cognitive decline is among the leading reasons people enter institutional care. Anything we can do to lower this risk will be of benefit.

The Nun Study

Over thirty years ago, a study called the Nun Study of Aging and Alzheimer's Disease was launched to examine the onset of Alzheimer's among a group of nuns. They seemed to be functionally just fine, but after they passed on, their brains were donated to the study and examined. The results showed indications that many of the nuns had Alzheimer's, yet they had not exhibited the signs of the disease while they were alive. How could the nuns have the disease but not show the signs? It is believed that some people are able to cope with it better than others by keeping their brains active and engaging socially in a meaningful way.

How can you stay meaningfully engaged?

You do so by staying involved in life. Volunteering, cultivating high-quality relationships, and being involved in social groups provide you with benefits that can improve your overall well-being.

The most well-known benefits include:

- Enhanced mental health that helps with a positive outlook on life
- A sense of belonging when doing something meaningful together
- Better self-esteem from contributing to others outside of yourself
- Improved physical health from better eating with friends and family
- Increased cognitive functioning by sharpening our minds with learning, processing, and responding to the world around us
- Accountability to stay well
- The cultivation of purposeful living by looking forward to interactions and gaining a sense of fulfillment

---

Studies show that regular social engagement may actually delay the onset of dementia symptoms. With all of these benefits, it should be clear that your social interaction is a crucial part of your health plan throughout your life.

An aspect of the studies to highlight is the benefit of how meaningful we find our interactions to be. For example, being engaged in religious or charitable organizations, civic groups, or other circles whose purpose has an impact on how you find meaning—any of these will have positive impacts on your health as well as a good way to expand the age range of your circle of friends. It is also important to recognize that we often make friends within our age-group, but this group shrinks as we age. So, it is vital to make friends with folks 5, 10, 15 or even more years younger than yourself.

How are you doing?

Take an honest look at your level of social interactions, then make decisions on how you can improve. Let's define how we rate social interactions:

- **Frequent**: You have daily, meaningful interactions with others. You have a network of people with whom you regularly interact.
- **Moderate**: You occasionally attend family gatherings or talk with neighbors, but lack deeper conversation and meaningful relationships.
- **Minimal**: You only engage in essential interactions. You only interact with a limited number of other individuals.

Whatever level you are, make a plan to move up to the next level by improving the quantity and quality of your social interactions.

Healthy Lifestyle: Socialize

My current meaningful social interactions are: (Select one)

- ☐ Frequent (daily meaningful interactions)
- ☐ Moderate (family and some social gatherings; somewhat superficial)
- ☐ Minimal (only essential interactions with others or with limited individuals)

My plan to increase meaningful social interactions includes: (Select all that apply)

- ☐ Volunteering in charitable/religious service
- ☐ Joining/engaging with hobby or civic groups
- ☐ Other

Notes regarding my Socialize Plan:

Gathering the Right Medical Team

Let's turn our attention to another way to be proactive when focusing on your healthcare: whom you select for your medical team.

There are two major categories to understand when building your ideal medical team.

- Look into the options provided **inside the Insurance System.**
  These include Board-Certified Geriatricians and other Geriatric Specialists.
- Explore the world of options **outside the Insurance System.**
  We refer to this as Private Pay, and it includes options that are focused on preventative care and wellness science.

When you look at the healthcare professionals you have on your team, you likely have a primary care physician or provider who is the quarterback of your medical team, supported by various specialists you may see for specific issues. The primary care physician is likely trained and board-certified for the adult population.

For children under 18, however, there is the pediatrician, because the physiology of children is different. Medicine and interventions appropriate for adults may often be harmful for children. A pediatrician, because of his or her education, is better suited to handle these nuances, and we do not hesitate to seek out a pediatrician for our children.

So even though we know that the physiology of adults over age 65 is different than the rest of the population, why do we make little attempt to try and seek out the specialist who may better understand these nuances?

There is an area of practice of specialists trained to better care for those people over 65—and it is called **Geriatrics**.

Chances are you already have a doctor with whom you have spent a considerable amount of time. They know you and your health history and you're comfortable with them. So why should you consider changing your doctor?

Consider these statistics for retirees who have switched to a Geriatrician as their primary physician:

- *56% fewer incidents of depression*
- *40% lower use of home health services*
- *33% less likelihood of becoming disabled*

These statistics reinforce the idea that as you age, you should seek the care of a Geriatrician as opposed to a traditional physician. As you age, there are many changes in your own body that you need to be aware of, and Geriatricians are knowledgeable about these changes. Geriatrics specialists are available to you after you turn age sixty-five. These physicians are covered by your insurance policy, so you will not need to spend any additional money seeking out their skill set.

Make it your business to seek out professionals who are better suited to help you with preventative and management of care needs.

Are you still unsure if you need a Geriatric Specialist?

The American Geriatrics Society (AGS) established the Beers Criteria® for Potentially Inappropriate Medication Use in Older Adults as guidelines for healthcare professionals to help improve the safety of prescribing medications.

Each year, the AGS publishes a list of medications that should not be given to seniors on a routine basis, unless absolutely necessary. It is called the Beers Drug List[1]. The drugs are classified into categories based on what they treat, such as blood pressure, pain, depression and insomnia. If these medications are prescribed to seniors, they should be under the strict supervision of a physician, such as a Geriatrician or an internist with a specialty in Geriatrics. And yet, each year, doctors who are unaware of the adverse effects on geriatric-age patients routinely prescribe these medications without any supervision.

A study from Brown University's Warren Alpert Medical School found that physicians prescribed drugs time and time again to older patients who were specifically advised not to take these drugs due to severe side effects, such as dizziness and falls, or the tendency of the drugs to stay in their systems far longer than prescribed.[2]

The study, which looked at six million men and women enrolled in Medicare Advantage plans, found that one out of five seniors were prescribed medications from drugs listed as high-risk for this age group[3].

That's 1 in 5...

And that's another good reason to find a Geriatrics Specialist.

1 American Geriatrics Society. (2018). American Geriatrics Society 2015 updated Beers Criteria® for potentially inappropriate medication use in older adults. Retrieved from https://www.guidelinecentral.com/summaries/american-geriatrics-society-2015-updated-beers-criteria-for-potentially-inappropriate-medication-use-in-older-adults/#section-420

2 Orenstein, D. (2013). <p>21% of U.S. elderly take high-risk medicines</p>. News from Brown, 401:863-1862. Retrieved from https://news.brown.edu/articles/2013/04/risk

3 Johns Hopkins Medicine. (n.d.). Specialists in aging: Do you need a Geriatrician? Retrieved from https://www.hopkinsmedicine.org/health/healthy_aging/healthy_connections/specialists-in-aging-do-you-need-a-geriatrician

Inside the Insurance System

Most insurance-based options focus on giving a diagnosis and treatment of illness, but you can use this same system to stay healthy in the first place. You'll need to know what kind of doctors are most knowledgeable regarding aging conditions. Then you'll learn how you can get insurance to cover these specialists.

Finding the right Geriatrician (finding a Geriatrician at all) can be difficult. When you start looking for one, start with an understanding of these four options:

1. **Geriatric Care Clinics**
2. **Board-Certified Geriatricians**
3. **Physicians Advertising as Geriatric Care Services**
4. **Other Medical Providers**

Let's explore each of these options.

1) Geriatric Care Clinics

This is your best option when choosing geriatric care. While stand-alone Geriatricians are subject to restrictions imposed by Medicare, Geriatric Care Clinics are not. They have entire teams of healthcare providers and staff who specialize and focus on geriatric care. These clinics offer a robust range of services focused on maintaining your health and recovery from illness episodes. Examples of these services include:

- Transportation to and from clinics, care/coach manager for each patient
- Short wait times but significantly longer time with the doctor
- 24-hour access to a doctor (or a nurse)
- Team approach
- Excellent coordination of additional social services

If this is the option you choose, find a true geriatric clinic by looking for the ones open only to Medicare-age patients and staffed with geriatric care-focused professionals.

2) Board-Certified Geriatrician

Another excellent option is a stand-alone Board-Certified Geriatrician.

The qualifications you should look for when selecting a Geriatrician are:

✓ **Board-Certified**

✓ **Accepting new patients**

✓ **Accepts your insurance**

✓ **Younger than you**

Finding a Geriatrician can be difficult, and you shouldn't be discouraged if it takes you some time to find one. There are many resources designed specifically to help you find Geriatricians in your area, including:

- Your insurance company website
- Medicare[1]
- The practitioner search function on American Board of Internal Medicine[2]
- American Board of Family Medicine[3]
- The American Geriatrics Society website[4]
- The AgingOptions Resource Guide

All physicians must deal with the restrictions set forth by insurance companies, namely that they are expected to see patients in high volume, which only allows them a small amount of time with each patient. While Board-Certified Geriatricians still have to deal with these limits, they are more able to offer you specialized care focused on health issues affecting patients ages 65 and older.

1 medicare.gov

2 abim.org

3 theabfm.org

4 americangeriatrics.org

3) Physician with Geriatric Specialty

Depending on your location, you may find that there just aren't many Geriatricians available. If this is the case, we suggest you find a physician who advertises as a geriatric care physician. While not board-certified, these physicians, in our experience, are adept at geriatric care and are dedicated to helping serve the older adult population because they have taken additional training in this area.

We suggest you interview a handful of physicians who identify as geriatric care physicians to make a more informed decision as to which physician can serve you best.

4) Other Medical Providers

If you are still unable to find a good geriatric care solution, we suggest you find an advanced registered nurse practitioner (ARNP) or a physician's assistant (PA) who has an education and background in geriatric care and is working under a physician with a similar background.

It is natural for your primary care physician to list all of the reasons you should remain with him or her. We suggest at least asking a Geriatrician about the benefits of switching. With a professional second opinion, you can then balance the discussions with the benefits you feel you will receive.

As you think about your geriatric care options, pause to answer the following questions.

Health: Geriatricians

My plan to gather the right Geriatric Care Team: (Select all that apply)

- ☐ I already have a Geriatric Care solution
- ☐ I need to locate Geriatric options near me
  - ☐ Geriatric Care Clinics
  - ☐ Board-Certified Geriatricians
  - ☐ Physicians, PAs, or ARNPs with geriatrics training
  - ☐ Undecided

Notes regarding my Geriatric Care Plans:

Outside the Insurance System

If your retirement income allows it, there are options outside of insurance-based healthcare.

Insurance-covered medical care is heavily managed and tends to prevent qualified physicians from having the freedom to really focus on preventative care. To fill this gap, there is an industry outside of the insurance premiums that caters to those who are willing to invest in their own health with a focus exclusively on preventative care. These doctors will not see you after you've had a heart attack or cancer, but they do whatever can be done to help you avoid having these conditions in the first place. Fascinating, isn't it?

These private pay healthcare clinics are stand-alone clinics run by doctors who prefer to operate outside of the typical healthcare system to avoid the restrictions placed by insurance companies. These restrictions usually prevent doctors from being able to administer or suggest treatments they believe are required simply because a patient's insurance doesn't cover it.

The shortcomings of insurance-covered medicine are not a secret to anyone. It is highly restrictive and leads to a frustrated healthcare community. This reality has led to doctors offering care for a fee outside of the insurance-covered care.

When you look at this option, you find that there are a few distinct models in the private pay world, including:

1. **Private/Preventative Care**
2. **Concierge Care**
3. **Wellness Science**

Let's discuss each option.

1) Private/Preventative Care

This type of clinic does not offer instant access to care, but instead focuses on long-term wellness and prescribing preventative care. For example, if you were diagnosed with cancer, they do not treat your cancer once you have it; their job is to help you avoid cancer in the first place.

One of the major advantages of preventative care clinics is that they often develop custom plans for your specific health needs that include diet, supplements, exercise, and other lifestyle plans to keep you healthy and prevent disease.

Another major benefit is that they focus on preventing serious health problems by looking for and diagnosing them early, sparing you the cost and problems that come with these diseases. Because they are not limited by insurance companies, Preventative Healthcare Clinics are able to serve a handful of clients (instead of being expected to fill a quota) and are therefore able to focus on a patient to a degree that mainstream clinics cannot. Because of this, their routine exams and health screenings are both more frequent and more thorough.

You may be surprised to discover that the major drawback to these types of clinics is not price, but availability. These clinics are in fact surprisingly affordable to those who consider themselves middle class. The difficulty comes in finding a clinic. An option to find one is by contacting the American Academy of Private Physicians. You can also reach out to AgingOptions for help, or access our resource guide to find any of the options you could be considering.

2) Concierge Care

A Concierge Physician is a primary care physician who handles a handful of cash-paying clients and will travel to meet you at your home or place of work, and will follow you to hospitals, etc.

3) Wellness Science

For those who find Concierge Care or Private-Pay Preventative Care Clinics too expensive and/or impractical, a new category of organizations is developing to fill the gap of preventative care. These are called Wellness Science. These companies usually offer virtual care and coordinate their work with local labs and providers. Generally, with such an organization, you will be linked to a 'wellness coach'—often a dietitian, who will be your day-to-day contact. This coach is backed by virtual physicians who read your charts and map out a strategy on how to keep you healthy. This knowledge is then relayed by the coach who will discuss health in a more comprehensive way and will motivate you, and hold you accountable.

Health: Private Pay Options

I plan to include the following Private Pay options in my Health team: (Select all that apply)

- ☐ Private/Preventative Care Clinics
- ☐ Concierge Care
- ☐ Wellness Science
- ☐ Undecided

Notes regarding my plan to include Private Pay options in my Health Team:

As you age you need to change the way you see health with a preventative point of view.

Wherever your choice of care leads, you must be actively involved in both your own personal health lifestyle, and in choosing those you entrust with your health. Selecting the right professionals for your medical team, ones whom you trust and who specialize in your specific health situation will drastically improve your ability to maintain your health.

It's true, your health is your greatest asset, and it requires your constant and active involvement. If you take time to eat right, exercise, socialize, and choose the right people for your medical team, your chances for a successful and happy retirement will improve dramatically.

Choosing Health Insurance: A Quick Primer

How do you work with your insurance professional to choose a plan that's right for you? The first step is to understand your options. You will have the option to either 1) enroll in traditional Medicare and a Medigap plan, or 2) enroll in a Medicare Advantage plan. You will see plenty of advertising for Medicare Advantage plans because these plans are offered by private insurance companies. You won't hear much about traditional Medicare. Medicare Advantage plans can be confusing to compare. There is no requirement that the companies all offer a similar set of benefits, as traditional Medicare plans do.

What to Look for in an Insurance Plan

When you're looking for a health insurance provider, your best bet is to choose a company that offers preventative care benefits. If a health insurance policy includes the following benefits, it's worth considering:

- Ability to see any doctor of your choice without having to get a primary care physician's referral
- Access to naturopaths
- Access to nutritionists
- Access to a gym membership
- Plan with no deductible (or a very small one) and no co-payments
- Plan with no requirement for you to fill out claim forms
- Access to a university-connected hospital
- No issue about in-network or out-of-network care. You should be covered nationwide the same as where you live.

NOTE: You may not find a policy that includes every benefit on this list, so choose one that offers as many as possible.

Tips for Choosing a Health Plan

For best results, consider a traditional Medicare plan with a Medigap policy. Expect to pay around $200/month for this coverage. If this is too much, a Medicare Advantage Plan is another option. If you go this route, choose a zero-premium plan. You won't be able to see any doctor you want (you'll be asked to choose one from their network). You will have deductibles and co-payments, and an out-of-pocket cap of about $7,500 or so. The advantage of this plan is that for every year you don't need heavy duty care, you will save about $2,400 a year. In the years you do need a lot of care, your out-of-pocket will be limited to about $7,500 a month.

A Medigap plan with a prescription drug plan will allow you the broadest coverage available. These plans will not give you dental, vision, or hearing coverage. The Medicare Advantage plans that do offer dental, vision, or hearing coverage don't offer much of a benefit. But, if you want to save money for now and go with a Medicare Advantage plan, know that in most states, if you want to switch from a Medicare Advantage plan to a traditional Medicare plan at some point in the future, you may be denied because companies can ask for medical underwriting.

Health: Choosing Health Insurance Coverage

I plan to explore the following health insurance coverage options: (Select all that apply)

- ☐ Traditional Medicare + Medigap Plan
- ☐ Medicare Advantage Plan

I plan to find health insurance coverage that features: (Select all that apply)

- ☐ Low (or no) deductible
- ☐ No claim form requirement
- ☐ No network requirement

I plan to find a health insurance plan that includes the following benefits: (Select all that apply)

- ☐ Access to the doctor of my choice
- ☐ Access to preventative care
- ☐ Access to nutritionists
- ☐ Access to a gym membership
- ☐ Access to a university-connected hospital

Notes regarding my plan to choose Health Insurance Coverage:

Housing Planning

For Your Retirement

As you go through this workbook, you will be getting more than just a plan for housing in retirement. Your plan for housing will be integrated with your plans for health, financial, and legal issues during the retirement years. There is no better foundation for a successful retirement.

Defining "Home"

From our memories and our loved ones to our safety and our belonging.... home is where the heart is.

And as we get older, we must also consider that home will need to be... where the *care* is.

That's what we will be focusing on in this chapter.

There is an eye-opening study from Stanford University on how people fare with their housing goals when they use traditional planning methods. And if you learn anything from the study, it is that although you may be hoping to live out the rest of your life in your own home, your chances of realizing this goal are about 30%.[1]

The chances that you will take your last breath in a hospital, hospice house, nursing home, or other institutional care setting—a place you hope never to end up—are 70%.

---

1 Centers for Disease Control and Prevention. (2016). QuickStats: Percentage distribution of deaths, by place of death – United States, 2000-2014 Retrieved from www.cdc.gov/mmwr/volumes/65/wr/mm6513a6.htm#suggestedcitation

No way did you hope or even expect this outcome, but it's just a reality because traditional planning simply does not address this issue in an effective manner. Generally speaking, other than having a strong desire to be able to live out one's life at home, there is little actual planning that most of us will have undertaken ahead of time. The first time most people confront the issue with any degree of seriousness will be after a health crisis befalls them, rendering them unable to manage their activities of daily living without assistance of others because of physical or cognitive impairment.

The bottom line is this: If you are like most Americans, you will find yourself facing this issue and likely discover that you do not have all that it takes to allow you to access care at home—at least without having to spend huge sums of money and running the risk of going broke.

Perhaps even more distressing will be seeing your loved ones become your unpaid caregivers, which neither of you desires, nor can it be done for any extended period of time without significant personal sacrifice on the part of your loved ones.

The good news is this: With proper *LifePlanning*, you should be able to not only hope for—but actually realize—a better outcome. You will avoid institutional care. You won't go broke. You won't become a burden on your loved ones.

The Cost of Not Having a Plan

A theme throughout our lives has been to plan. It has been a watchword for all of us whether at work or play, going out to dinner or going to the doctor. So why, at this important point in our lives, do we minimize this strategic activity that will have such an impact on not just our life but on so many others?

Stanford University's School of Medicine Home Hospice program has found that only 24% of Americans put their wishes for care in writing. Another 16% have thought about how they want to be cared for but haven't done anything about it. Even worse, 19% have never even considered the question.[1]

1 Bailey, A., & Periyakoil, V.J. (n.d.). Where do Americans die? Stanford School of Medicine/Palliative Care. (A. Bailey states data is "~10 years old", personal communications, November, 2018). Retrieved from https://palliative.stanford.edu/home-hospice-home-care-of-the-dying-patient/where-do-americans-die/

When aging people face a health crisis they have not planned for and a housing decision comes into play, it is probably too late. Chances are that at this point these aging people will lack the mental ability to make sound decisions concerning their housing situation. Putting off the decision means inadvertently deciding that someone else must choose their outcome.

Planning your housing in advance and putting your wishes in writing creates a much higher likelihood that you will live out your life in your own home.

When you have not planned your housing future and have to deal with incapacity, regardless of the circumstances, conflict will arise and perhaps in unexpected ways. Given that humans tend to age slowly, it is easy for us to discount the extent of our own incapacities and to misperceive ourselves as healthy. By doing this, it puts our loved ones in the uncomfortable position of trying to convince us that our desire to age in our own home may be inappropriate.

You may see yourself as healthy enough to age in place, but there is a high probability that you're unaware of—or doggedly unwilling to admit—your true condition. We see this in nearly every single case where a child seeks our help. Either the parent is unsafe at home and stubbornly refuses to move, or was moved to a care setting but is upset and insists on returning home. Meanwhile, the children are bewildered and seeking not only options, but ways to reassure their parent that their safety and interests are their highest priority.

Avoiding the Conflict

Your role is to create a plan to avoid these frustrations and also to avoid the high cost of future moves due to health challenges and the related financial costs by understanding the issues from a more rational point of view. Once you fully comprehend what aging in place entails and you are aware of the resources you will need to reach your goal successfully without facing financial difficulty or burdening others, you might want to take the time to courageously examine alternative ways of aging. Bravely consider options that are healthier for all parties.

The Housing Decision Process

If asked today, "*what is your housing plan?*"

...your answer would probably be something like,

"*I plan on living my life out in my own home* ***as long as I possibly can****, and when the day comes that I am unable to manage the house or my health fails me, I will figure something out.*"

This may sound like a logical and rational plan, but in reality it is anything but logical or rational.

And here is why:

Think of what life will likely look like the day you are not able to care for the house or your health has failed you! You may have fallen down and broken your hip; or the fog of memory loss is making life confusing and challenging. The place you will find the most comfort at this time in your life, on what arguably will be the worst day in your life, is in the familiarity of your home.

But, instead, you are planning on moving on that day, thereby condemning yourself to compounding your misery by moving to a place where you know no one, you have no control over your life, and everyone will be barking out orders. All because you thought it sounded good to agree to a move when living at home became impossible. Know that at that time, no matter what you say now, you likely will pitch a fit and not want to move—turning the issue into a total nightmare for your loved ones.

Let's look at this issue a bit differently. When you say you want to live out your life in your home, more likely you are saying that you do not desire to move when your health fails you. You wish for the care to come to you. You don't want to be moved to a place of care on what may be the worst day of your life.

So why would you want to consider a program called *LifePlanning*? The answer: Because it provides predictability of the outcome.

With *LifePlanning*, you can significantly improve your odds of staying out of institutional care and access care in the home of your choosing without becoming a burden on your loved ones, or taking the chance of running out of money.

The first step in this planning process is defining what the term "home" means to you.

What do you picture when you think of the word "home"?

Most people will visualize the place where they are living. But, if you desire to have the care come to you when you face incapacity, then describing the place you are currently living as home, without more, will prove to be the wrong way to define the term home.

The word "home" in retirement should mean that you are living in a place when you still have about eight to ten years of good health ahead of you[1], where you have assurance that if you face incapacity, the care will come to you—you will not have to move to a place of care.

The setting can be any place—your current home, a more appropriate home, a mother-in-law unit in your child's home, or a retirement community. You just need the assurance that you will not be moved when your health fails you.

The issue then becomes one of timing. For many, that's around the age of 75.

1 R. Nagaich states, "Familiarity takes about 10 years... make the move by mid-70's of if you think you have 10 healthy years ahead", based on 17 years of elder law practice (personal communications, November, 2018).

There are only two options you will really have to pick from:

1. **Live in a private residence**
2. **Live in a retirement community**

How do you make that decision?

In the end, here is what it boils down to: What do you want to avoid more: being a burden on loved ones, or moving to a retirement community? That is a hard choice. Let's see if we can help make that decision easy to understand.

---

1. You can live in a private residence, such as your home or with a loved one.

- You will likely leave a bigger inheritance to your children.
- BUT—you will be more reliant on their support. So, you will not be able to say that you don't mind being a burden on your children. You can minimize the burden —not eliminate it. This is because when caregivers are hired, someone will need to be there to make sure that you are not being taken advantage of or being neglected. That is a role you cannot take away from your family.

2. On the other hand, living in a retirement community will have two distinct advantages:

- You will certainly be less of a burden to your children and loved ones when you are incapacitated.
- If you are married, upon your incapacity or death, your spouse will not have to face isolation or establish a new circle of people to be around.
- BUT—you will be spending your children's inheritance.

Housing pre-planning in your *LifePlan* will guide you through a set of decisions about where you want to end up (what we call your Forever home) and how you should allocate your resources to support those decisions. For now, try to keep an open mind about all of the possibilities.

It's good to know the details behind both options as Housing is your most important decision. Let's take a look at both and weigh the pros and cons, starting with a Private Residence.

Requirements for Selecting a Private Residence

Our current home is the option most of us have in mind for our retirement years. We imagine that we will live in our existing home until we pass away or until we're required to move for health reasons.

While aging in place may seem like a simple enough decision, it comes with many considerations and requirements to ensure that you are safe, well-cared-for, and in close proximity to all the services and individuals you will need in your later years. Remember, the goal here is that you will be able to stay in this home all the way until the end, which means you need to envision what it will take to receive care in this home.

The requirements are:

1. **Age-Friendly Home (both structure and location)**
2. **Financial Resources (to provide aid in this home if required)**
3. **Family/Social Support (to oversee your care when the time comes)**

Let's take a look at those requirements.

1) Age-Friendly Home: Structure & Location

There are a couple of aspects to consider when evaluating the private residence where you are going to live in your later years. You'll want to be assured that you can live here safely when you are older, or if you develop an illness or medical condition. Homes that address these considerations effectively are called "Age-Friendly." To see if your residence of choice is Age-Friendly, take a look at the structure itself, and the neighborhood where the home is located.

▸ First of all, the residence needs to be Age-Friendly.

Whether or not your home is Age-Friendly comes down to a few main features. One great reference for the structural features of an Age-Friendly home are the rules of Universal Design. Think about the home you have in mind. Does it include these features?

- ☐ No-step entries
- ☐ Single-floor living, which eliminates the need to navigate stairs
- ☐ Switches and outlets reachable at any height
- ☐ Extra-wide hallways and doors to accommodate wheelchairs
- ☐ Lever-style door and faucet handles

These features ensure that it is safe to remain in your home while you age. Unfortunately, it is estimated that only 1% of homes in America have these five basic features that make a home Age-Friendly.[1]

▸ The next thing to consider is if your home is in an Age-Friendly neighborhood.

Try to imagine these considerations in a future where you may be slowing down or more vulnerable.

- ☐ Do you feel safe walking around?
- ☐ Are medical facilities nearby?
- ☐ Are emergency responders readily available?
- ☐ Are grocery stores and drugstores conveniently located?

1 Joint Center for Housing Studies of Harvard University. (2014). Housing America's older adults- Meeting the needs of an aging population. Retrieved from www.jchs.harvard.edu/sites/default/files/jchs-housing_americas_older_adults_2014_1.pdf

2) Financial Resources to Stay at Home

Making sure your home is adequately equipped and ideally located isn't the only consideration when it comes to deciding where to live. Equipping your home (or relocating to a more appropriate home) takes money, and it takes money to pay the people who will be helping with your health and home care as well.

While there are several factors that determine the final amount required, there are also several unknowns.

Unknown factors include:

- **How much care will you need?**
- **For how long?**
- **At what level?**

The absolute best thing you can do to address these unknowns and determine what will be necessary to achieve this goal will be a Financial Dashboard. This is covered thoroughly in the Financial section.

Now, this may make it sound like you'll need enormous savings to be able to age at home, but we're here to say, you don't. Like all the other aspects of aging, all it takes is the right pre-planning to be successful. You can age at home with limited assets, but you'll need to understand how your various private assets and public benefits all work and intersect.

3) Family / Social Support

The final requirement to successfully age in a private residence is the support of your friends and family (or a care manager if friends and family aren't available. More on this professional later). These are people who know your wishes and your goals, and will work to ensure these are met when you fall ill or become incapacitated. Remember: if you're planning to stay in your home (and age in place), you'll likely need to bring care into your private residence. Who will make sure that you will not be neglected or be taken advantage of?

Someone will need to properly utilize your assets to support your care; hire good, trustworthy caregivers; and provide oversight—and that means committed to checking in frequently.

It is very important to calculate the physical distance between yourself and those whose support you will need... friends, family, siblings, or your children. Many retirees fail to consider this aspect. A dream home in Hawaii doesn't do you much good when your children, who are supposed to be your primary caregivers, live in Germany. Living close means their availability and support can be counted on and also minimizes the burden you place on them in times of crisis. We recommend that you live less than five miles away from someone you trust, and who will check on you daily if you are receiving care in your home.

Choosing to live in a private residence will inevitably put a burden on your loved ones. This is due to their more active role in your care than if you were to live at a retirement community. Whether they are in charge of overseeing your caretakers, ensuring that your home is age-friendly, or they are your primary direct caregiver, aging-in-place will likely add additional burden.

Consider forms of compensation for the loved ones who provide care on a regular, prolonged basis. This topic will be covered again in section Four–Legal Planning.

Geriatric Care Manager

As you plan your support, we recommend seeking out a Geriatric Care Manager for times of emergency. These professionals will be able to coordinate services in your time of need, and are specifically designed for the purpose of arranging care in whatever setting you determine, including your own home.

Imagine a scenario where you have a fall and end up in the hospital. After patching you up, the doctors and nurses know you will need some more assistance. Your Power of Attorney probably is there at your bedside when the discharge nurse asks which rehab center you would like to be transported to. Without proper planning by you, your POA will likely answer, "We don't know" and asks for a recommendation, which the nurse by law is not allowed to give. Your Power of Attorney might just pick a random rehab center and you end up in what is essentially a nursing home. At that point, if either of you tried to insist on going back home, the hospital staff simply could not allow it, since they have a responsibility for your improved health.

Now instead, imagine that at the discharge moment, your Power of Attorney calls your predetermined Geriatric Care Manager. This person comes to the hospital, reviews your chart, and tells the doctors "this patient wants to rehabilitate in their home. Based on the medical chart, if we arrange for this type of equipment, home improvements, and care providers over the next few weeks, their home will be safe and acceptable, right?" Now, the hospital staff is more likely to agree to this arrangement and you're back in your home! We will cover how to write this professional team member into your plan in the Legal Section.

We've covered a lot here so let's pause and get your thoughts on living in a private residence:

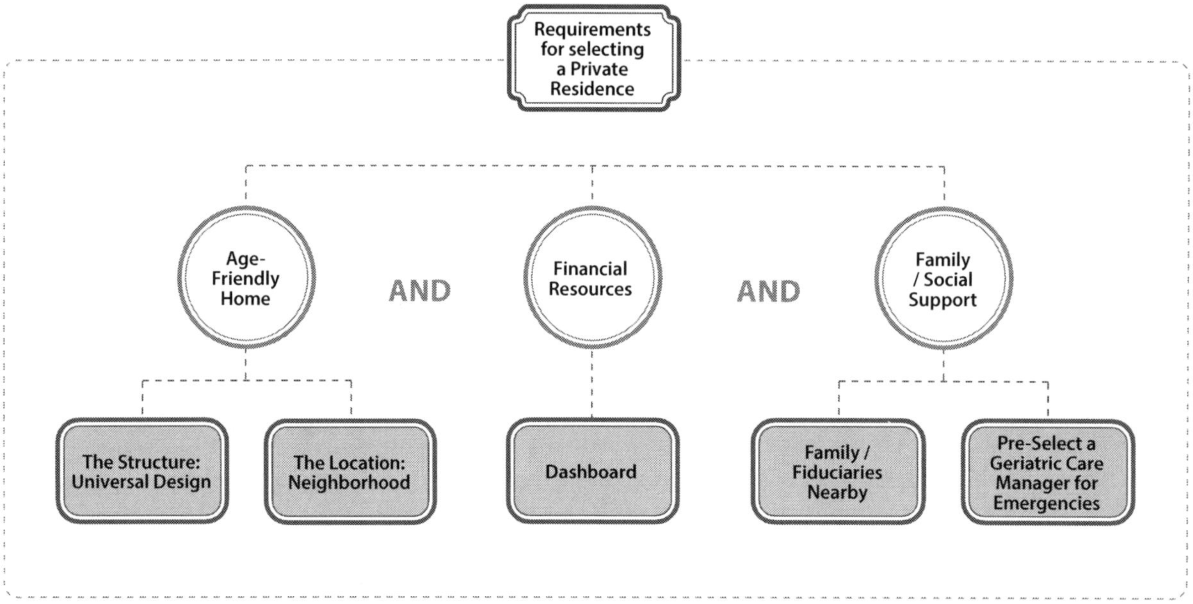

Housing: Requirements to Age in a Private Residence

I am interested in aging in a Private Residence:

- ☐ (**If yes**) My residence will meet the following requirements:
    - ☐ I will live in an Age-Friendly Home (the home and the location)
    - ☐ I have the Financial resources. (I can cover the cost of living at home and pay for care as needed.)
    - ☐ I have localized Family/Social support (Fiduciaries are within 5 miles and I will acquire a Geriatric Care Manager)
- ☐ (**If no**) See Retirement Community Options

Notes regarding my ability to age in a Private Residence:

Private Residence Options

Aging-in-Place can seem like a one-choice decision (you either age in your current home or you don't), but in fact there are still other options depending on how you define "home."

There are a few different Private Residence scenarios to consider if your goal is to age away from a retirement community. Using the "Requirements for Selecting a Private Residence" as your guide, let's explore the different Age-in-Place options.

Remain in Current Home

Option One is the one we all think of... remaining at home, with all of its comforts and familiarity. But with only 1% of homes fully equipped to be Age-Friendly,[1] will your current house be able to accommodate your needs throughout the rest of your life?

Move to a New Age-Friendly Home

Option Two is to move into a new home specifically built to be Age-Friendly. These homes will have all of the necessities required for safety and convenience for older adults. Ideally this move occurs by the time you are age 75. By moving to this type of home well ahead of major healthcare needs, you are then able to build familiarity and comfort with your new forever home.

Move In with Loved Ones

Another option to consider when planning to avoid institutional care is moving in with a family member. Many Americans overlook this option, but it certainly qualifies as

1 Joint Center for Housing Studies of Harvard University. (2014). Housing America's older adults- Meeting the needs of an aging population. Retrieved from www.jchs.harvard.edu/sites/default/files/jchs-housing_americas_older_adults_2014_1.pdf

remaining in a private residence, which many desire. In addition, it can be invigorating to be surrounded by younger housemates.

Moving in with a family member has many advantages, but it also comes with its own challenges. It essentially guarantees that you will be burdening your loved ones to some degree, but in spite of that, this option also allows you to be close to family and protect your assets from certain long-term care expenses.

If you're planning to incorporate potential Medicaid benefits, there is something to keep in mind when moving in with a loved one. Medicaid has an infamous "five-year lookback" rule that usually disqualifies you from Medicaid benefits if you've transferred any assets out of your name in the last five years. However, when planning on moving in with a loved one, there are some specific allowances that can help shorten or eliminate this rule.

Move to a Lifestyle Community

Finally, there is the option to move to a Lifestyle Community. These are considered by some to be more of a leisure community as opposed to a retirement community. Most commonly, these are the 55+ neighborhoods, where you still live in an age-friendly private residence, though there are some additional amenities offered. The focus of these communities is to create a shared space where aging residents can maintain social lives and healthy lifestyles. These places value meaningful connections and a sense of home and belonging within their communities.

Let's pause to plan if you prefer to retire in a private residence option, and if so, which one.

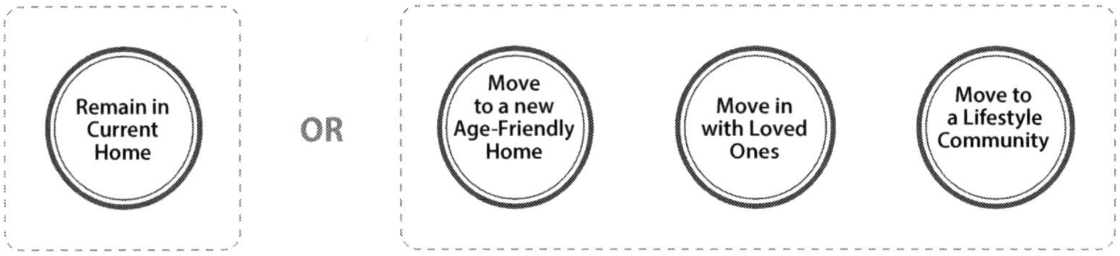

Housing: Private Residence Options

Select the options that reflect your preferences and make notes about what you would like to focus on regarding this topic.

My interest in Private Residence options:

- ☐ I am not considering a Private Residence
- ☐ I am interested in living in a Private Residence

The Private Residence housing options I'm considering include:

- ☐ N/A
- ☐ Remain in my current home
- ☐ Move to a new Age-Friendly home
- ☐ Move in with Loved Ones
- ☐ Move to a Lifestyle Community

Universal Design review for the home of my choosing: (if applicable)

- ☐ I plan to review the Universal Design for each home I'm considering

Notes regarding my Private Residence choice:

Retirement Community Options

For those who do not wish to (or cannot) live out life in a private residence, the other major option we can discuss is living in a retirement community.

Retirement communities these days offer substantially more than in the past, providing retirees a much greater opportunity to maintain a social life and also sometimes allowing easier and less-expensive access to many of the services you need when you age.

Although selecting a retirement community that suits you may seem daunting at first, we believe that the single most important consideration is that the retirement home offer you contractual assurance (in writing) that upon moving into the community, you will never be asked to move out—whether due to depleted funds or increased care because of deteriorating health.

Verbal assurances are inadequate, as only written assurances stand up in court. Our advice here is centered around ensuring that you not only select a retirement community that is perfect for your needs, but also that you will not have to move again.

Retirement communities fall into two broad categories:

- **Life Plan Communities**, also known as Continuing Care Retirement Communities (CCRCs)
- *Everything Else* (Independent Living, Assisted Living, Memory Care, Adult Family Home, Nursing Home, etc.)

While all of the communities seek to serve the aging population, only CCRCs can offer the written assurance that once you move to that community, you will never have to move again no matter your financial or health situation.

Approach these options much like you would if planning to stay in a Private Residence. Your financial plan needs to accommodate paying to bring care into one of these settings when/should you need it.

Retirement communities that do not accept Medicaid or a similar program as a source of payment should be crossed off your list of considerations because they will not be able or willing to accommodate changes to your health or finances. The goal here is to plan your affairs so that you won't have to move again when your health fails or your finances run dry.

In many instances, a community may offer more than one of the following options. In those cases, an important question to ask is whether you would need to move from one part of the community to another in order to access that category of care.

Retirement Community options include:

1. **Independent Living**
2. **Assisted Living**
3. **Memory Care**
4. **Residential Care Homes (Adult Family Homes)**
5. **Skilled Nursing Facilities (Nursing Homes)**
6. **Life Plan Communities (CCRCs)**

Let's first understand the community options that do not typically offer a guarantee about staying there. In many instances, a community may require you to move relative to increasing levels of care needs, either from one part of the community to another, or from one community to an entirely different option.

Finally, we will discuss the option designed to be inclusive for all your potential needs.

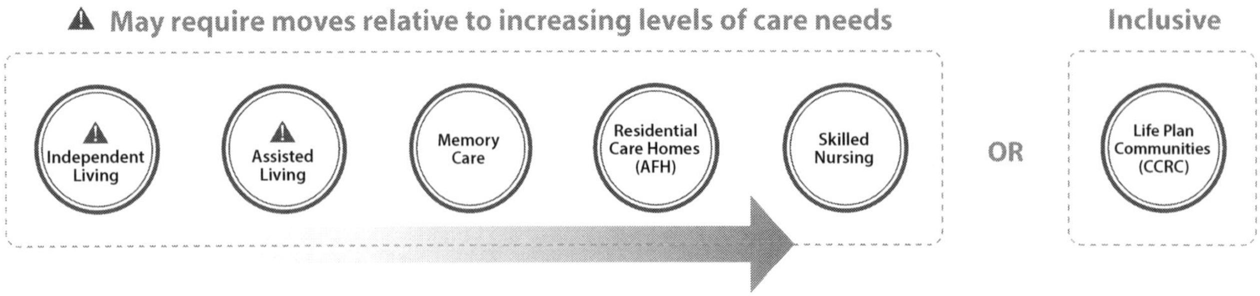

Independent Living

These communities are for older adults who are able to function independently and do not require any assistance for day-to-day activities and needs.

Independent Living, sometimes referred to as Adult Residential Care facilities, are housing arrangements offered specifically to seniors. They are often smaller homes with easy access and they eliminate the need to do yard work or maintenance. These homes offer independent housing to seniors, but also generally offer amenities, activities, and services, such as clubhouses so that residents can socialize with neighbors in the community.

An Independent Living facility is an option for aging persons who wish to age in a community, but prefer to live independently.

Be advised, unless you have made other arrangements for care, this option will likely require a move if you become ill or incapacitated.

Assisted Living

These communities are for those who need some assistance during their day-to-day activities, such as bathing, medication monitoring, or toileting, but do not need 24/7 care or assistance.

Be advised, unless you have made other arrangements for care, this option will likely require a move if you become ill or incapacitated.

Memory Care

Memory care facilities are for those with cognitive decline and need 24/7 care and assistance for their own safety. These establishments specialize in caring for people who suffer from Alzheimer's and other forms of dementia. Memory Care facilities go further than standard assisted living facilities by providing care that is specific to those with some form of dementia. This type of care typically includes 24-hour supervised care for patients.

Memory Care should be sought out when you or a loved one can no longer safely live at home due to any type of dementia, and desire a safe, specialized spectrum of care.

Residential Care Homes (Adult Family Homes)

Residential Care Homes, or Adult Family Homes. These are homes licensed to provide services and care to a small number of elderly adults (usually between six or eight).

These settings are typically a relatively large house with individuals residing in the bedrooms. Their services include personal care, specialized home health care, and room and board. Specific services and care options vary with each location. For instance, some offer specialized care for those with dementia, or they may have a nurse practitioner present on a regular basis.

Residential Care Homes are often the final location of someone who winds up there by surprise after a crisis strikes. When selecting an Adult Family Home, make sure you match the services with your particular current or projected care requirements. If they don't offer care for your unique requirements, you may be required to move to another facility.

Skilled Nursing Facilities (Nursing Homes)

These facilities are for people who do not need to be hospitalized, but cannot be cared for at home.

Most nursing homes have 24/7 caregivers and skilled nurses available to care for those with chronic illness, disabilities, or cognitive conditions. They basically provide assistance to activities of daily living (ADLs) and some health monitoring on a day-to-day basis.

These facilities may also house rehabilitation beds and departments.

Nursing homes are never a planned destination, but they are a common final residence for older adults who have encountered a health crisis. It often requires professional assistance in the form of a Geriatric Care Manager in order to check out of a nursing home or rehab center once admitted.

Now let's learn about the inclusive category.

Life Plan Communities (CCRCs)

Life Plan Communities, also known as Continuing Care Retirement Communities or CCRCs, are intended as a forever home community.

CCRCs offer a wide spectrum of care, ensuring that your needs are met whatever they are. One of the biggest benefits is that you are never isolated for health reasons or because of the passing of a spouse.

There are a few drawbacks, including the fact that you are essentially renting with a large financial investment, meaning that you will likely be spending more in this setting than in a house.

If you are contemplating moving to a CCRC, then you should know about the different contracts available and choose what best fits your needs. Let's review them:

Type A – Extensive or Lifecare Contract:

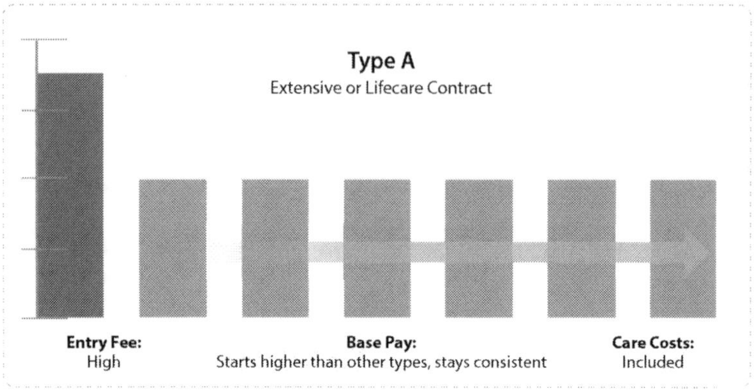

This contract requires a substantial entry fee, but sets a fairly stable monthly fee that will not change should you move to higher levels of care. This contract also likely has you paying more monthly than the other contracts, but should you require long-term advanced healthcare, will offer you financial stability. Under this contract, should your finances run dry and you are unable to pay, the CCRC will use the entrance fee you paid as collateral to cover the costs of living in the community. Finally, upon the death of the contract holder, part of the entry fee will be refunded to the heirs (the final details of that refund differ between communities).

Type B – Modified Contract:

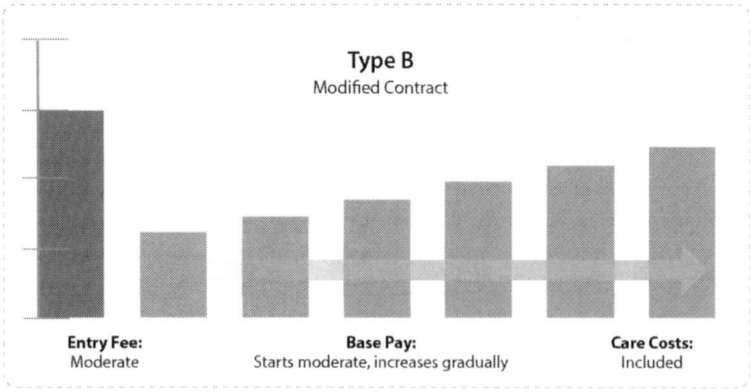

This contract also requires an entry fee and produces a stable monthly cost (usually the same or lower than communities offering type A contracts), but the difference is that you are only allowed a specified number of days at each level of care at the contracted rate before the rates are raised to market levels. This is good for most retirees since they usually face incapacity for a relatively short period of time and will not exceed the specified number of days. However, should your advanced long-term care regularly exceed the specified days, you may find yourself paying more than if you were to go with a type A contract.

Type C – Fee-for-Service Contract:

Like the other contracts, type C contracts require an entry and monthly fee, but typically at a noticeably lower price than the previous two contract types. The caveat here is that you pay for additional services on an as-needed basis. Although you pay market price for these services, you benefit from often receiving priority or guaranteed admission for services.

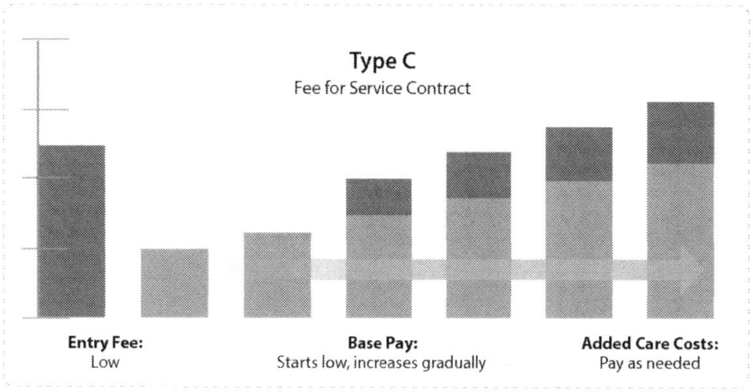

Type D – Rental Agreement Contract:

Instead of an entry fee, this contract allows you to rent your independent apartment in the community for a monthly fee. Similar to type C contracts, you also pay for additional services as needed at market price.

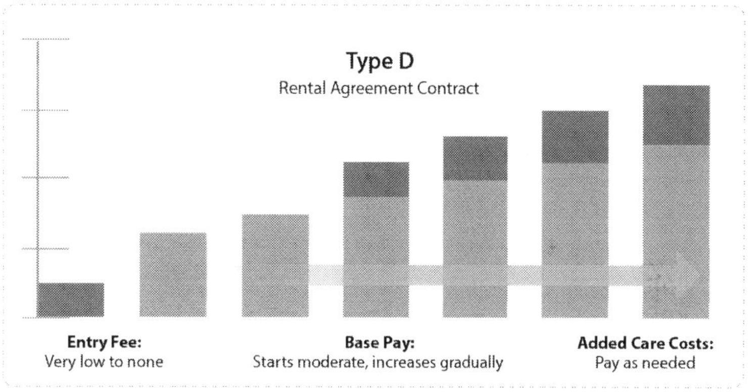

Type E – Equity Agreement Contract:

Finally, this contract is much like the rental option, but you actually purchase your independent apartment in the community just like you would a house or condo. Like some of the other contracts, you still pay a monthly fee or home owners association fee for the community amenities, and you would pay for additional services as needed at the market price.

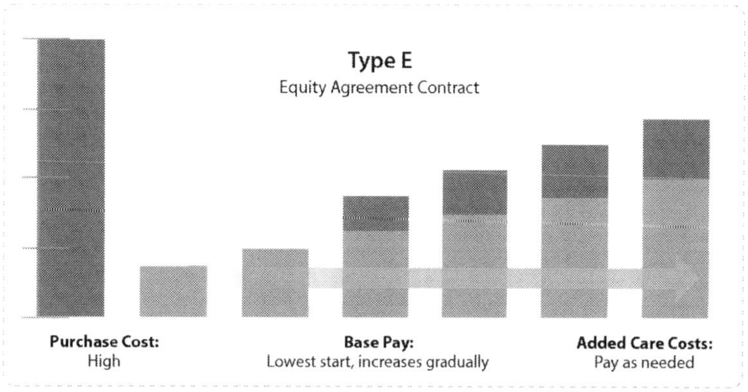

Now that you have had an opportunity to learn more about the retirement community options, think about how you would answer the following:

Housing: Retirement Community Options

My interest in Retirement Community options:

☐ I am not considering moving to a Retirement Community

☐ I am interested in moving to a Retirement Community

The Retirement Community options I'm considering are:

☐ N/A

☐ Independent Living

☐ Assisted Living

☐ Memory Care

☐ Residential Care Home (Adult Family Home)

☐ Skilled Nursing Facility

☐ Life Care Communities (CCRCs)

  ☐ I prefer a Type A – Extensive or Lifecare Contract

  ☐ I prefer a Type B – Modified Contract

  ☐ I prefer a Type C – Fee-for-Service Contract

  ☐ I prefer a Type D – Rental Agreement Contract

  ☐ I prefer a Type E – Equity Agreement Contract

☐ Undecided

Notes regarding my Retirement Community options: (Include areas of concern)

Family Meeting

After learning about the previous areas, those who desired to age in place may have only confirmed their desire to stay away from retirement communities. Others will take a look at CCRCs and decide that it isn't as bad as they imagined and could see themselves living in those types of communities.

Whatever decision you are leaning toward, do not act without first seriously analyzing your options, desires, and life situations. We advise that you set up a formal meeting with your family to discuss your housing options and decisions before you move forward with your decision.

After having seriously analyzed your options, it is time to have a formal family meeting. Section Five, Family Planning, discusses best-practices for how to prepare and hold family meetings.

We at AgingOptions recognize that this is a very lengthy and emotional process. After having carefully analyzed all of your options, taken a detailed look into what you want, and after having your family meeting, you are now prepared to make your final decision about housing.

We would like to remind you that housing can be boiled down to two decisions:

1. Private Residence

2. Retirement Community

Upon looking into both options, their pros and cons, and deciding which one will help you best achieve the goal of a forever home, then you've discovered the choice that is best for your personal housing plan.

Again, housing is your most important decision when it comes to retirement planning. Unlike the Health pillar where some decision choices are made daily, the housing decision is designed to happen just once.

The most critical question to consider as you finalize this choice is this: Can you confidently envision receiving any type of care you may eventually need in this home—wherever that is. If not, then you have not finalized this decision yet. This is a big one, so take your time.

Financial Planning

For Your Retirement

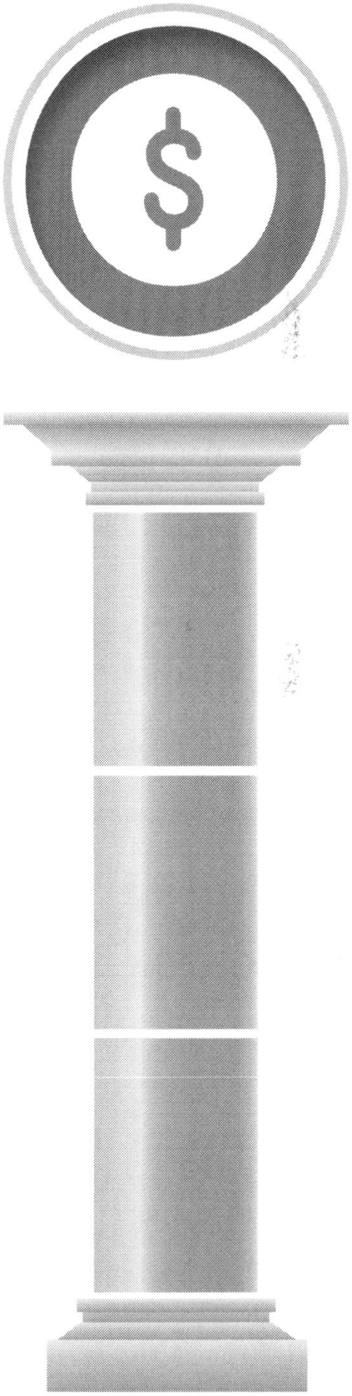

When it comes to your finances, AgingOptions' goal is not to give you investment advice. It is to help you protect your assets so that as you age, you do not end up broke and struggling. To be clear, having a lot of money doesn't guarantee you'll avoid institutional care. How you plan, manage, protect, and entrust your money to the right people is far more important than the amount of money you have.

It is not only important to have your financial decisions in order, but it is also critical that you provide the right guidance to your named agents clearly documented, so they know what outcomes to shoot for and what resources to utilize to help you realize your goals, when you can no longer manage your own affairs.

Your fiduciaries will be expected to carry out your wishes and manage your assets when you are no longer able to make your own decisions. The financial decisions you make now will go a long way toward securing not only your assets but also your peace of mind and quality of life as you age. So, too, will this knowledge minimize the burdens others will have to bear.

Your finances will not just magically manage themselves when a crisis arises, and things will not simply fall into the right places when the time comes. You need to build your own financial plan to ensure that your assets are utilized the way you want them to be.

Develop a Financial Dashboard

Whether you are working or retired, you are more than likely considering the rest of your life. Like most people, do you share the fear of outliving your resources? What financial expenditures are you expecting to deal with in retirement?

How you use your money is more important than how much money you have. Understanding the key principles of making successful financial decisions starts with creating a Financial Dashboard. A Financial Dashboard illustrates how much money it takes for you to be able to maintain your quality of life, looks ahead for pitfalls and dangers, and indicates whether you need to make adjustments to the way you are approaching your finances.

A Financial Dashboard is created by a Financial Planner using modeling software for the task. It's complicated and takes specialized knowledge, which makes it difficult for you to tell whether it was done well or not.

We will help you understand the process enough to feel familiar; then we will cover the types of questions your Financial Dashboard should be answering. This arms you with the confidence to tell when your Financial Planner is doing enough to guide you with a Dashboard tool.

Developing a dashboard is a three-step process:

1. **Expense Projections**
2. **Income Projections**
3. **Scenarios**

Let's explore each step.

1) Expense Projections

The first step is gaining a clear understanding of how much it costs to maintain your current quality of life or the one you want to live.

1. Take a look at your expenses over the past several months and average them by month or by year. We all have spending patterns, and if you think back over the years, you may find that every six or twelve months a new, unexpected expense comes up that seems unlike any other—but the amount and frequency are often similar. This average will give you a clear understanding of how much it costs to maintain your quality of life.
2. Then, note those expenses that remain the same by contract (for example, a mortgage, or an insurance premium).
3. Also note any expenses that will end after a certain number of years, such as a loan payment.

Each of these details will be helpful for a Financial Planner as they are projecting your spending into the future.

2) Income Projections

The next step to creating your Financial Dashboard is to determine where your income is coming from. Most retirees will have Social Security, pensions, or investments as their sources of income. Social Security and pension income are easily determined as they are fixed each month. Once you determine your fixed income, you will have a clear understanding of how much you need from your investments to maintain your quality of life.

Not all of your income from investments will come from your gains; some may be from the principal. That can be just fine—it all depends on your specific scenario. This also means that the more you draw from your nest egg, the less base there is for a return. You can find plenty of generalized "wisdom" on the Internet, but it is much more useful if you create a model of your own unique situation, with the help of a qualified Financial Planner, and make good decisions based on that information.

3) Scenarios

Having accomplished a baseline to your Financial Dashboard and a clearer view of your finances in front of you, it will be time to add important layers and to make the model thorough.

The purpose of this is to project enough "What If" scenarios to give you perspective and understanding. This will help you make decisions now that will set you up for success over time.

The first thing to insist on is adding a scenario for long-term care expenses in the future. This should be for yourself and your spouse if you are married. These expenses can range from $3,000 to as much as $18,000 per month, and may last a short while or several years. Without these possibilities put into the plan, these costs may blindside you in the future and derail all of your hard work.

After running these scenarios, you should insist on an analysis of any of the following questions that pertain to your situation:

- ✓ When is the ideal time to retire?
- ✓ When should I start Social Security benefits?
- ✓ How can I best maximize Social Security benefits?
- ✓ Should I invest in a long-term care insurance policy or not?
- ✓ If so, should it be a traditional policy, an asset-based policy, or a hybrid?
- ✓ Should I convert my traditional IRA accounts to Roth IRA accounts?
- ✓ How should I invest my assets?

Include any other questions that are unique to you.

Select a Financial Planner

When looking for professionals to help you develop your Financial Dashboard, there are certain things to consider. If you have a Financial Planner you trust completely, then you can ask that person to develop your Dashboard for you. If not, take into consideration the following:

- That person should have the Certified Financial Planner (CFP) credentials, which require rigorous study of these topics for certification.
- You should connect well with the Financial Planner on a personal level.
- He or she should be willing to provide advice with either a flat fee or on an hourly basis.

There are two compensation models for financial planning:

Fee-Only

These planners are generally free from commissions, and, in our opinion, better positioned to give you more objective advice. Fee-only planners charge either a flat fee or an hourly fee.

Fee-Based

These planners receive a percentage of the total assets they manage in your account, much like a commission, but are also able to charge other fees.

Generally, these planners are limited to investment options offered by the companies they work for. This can cause a conflict of interest when the planner is aware of options outside of their company that would be more beneficial to you, but they are unable to offer you access to those options.

Fee-based planners are not a bad option, but it can be difficult to differentiate between the varying qualities of fee-based planners.

Pause here to think about these initial steps in your financial planning.

Make notes about what you'd like to focus on, or cross out anything that you know does not apply.

Financial: Dashboard Decisions

My Financial Dashboard Decision: (Select one)

☐ I am confident with my current Financial Plan

☐ I would like to create/review my Financial Plan

My Financial Dashboard will provide the following information: (Select all that apply)

☐ When is the ideal time to retire?

☐ When should I start Social Security benefits?

☐ How can I best maximize Social Security benefits?

☐ Should I invest in a long-term care insurance policy or not? If so, should it be a traditional policy, an asset-based policy, or a hybrid?

☐ Should I convert my traditional IRA accounts to Roth IRA accounts?

☐ How should I invest my assets?

☐ Other: (Note below)

My Financial Planner Decisions: (Select one)

☐ I have a Financial Planner that I like

☐ I would like to speak with a new Financial Planner

☐ I'm undecided

Notes regarding my Dashboard and Financial Planner:

Address Uncovered Long-Term Care Costs

Dealing with uncovered medical or long-term care costs is one of the biggest difficulties one faces when aging. This issue is particularly threatening if your estate is valued under $1.5 million or you possess less than $1 million in liquid assets. While most people expect Medicare to cover all of their cost-related issues, the sad truth is that Medicare only covers acute care, and leaves long-term care costs virtually uncovered.

On top of that, long-term care costs are very high and rising fast. As mentioned earlier, costs throughout the United States can range from $3,000 to $18,000 per month depending on the level of care, and these expenses have risen nearly three times the rate of inflation. It is crucial to factor these costs into your plan.

There are a number of resources that can be used to pay for long-term care costs, and they are largely determined by your financial resources. **You may incorporate more than one option** into your financial plan. Let's take a look at the three payment categories for long-term care.

1. **Private pay (directly from your personal finances)**
2. **Long-Term Care Insurance (Private Pay)**
3. **Public Assistance**

Each approach is unique, so we will discuss them one at a time.

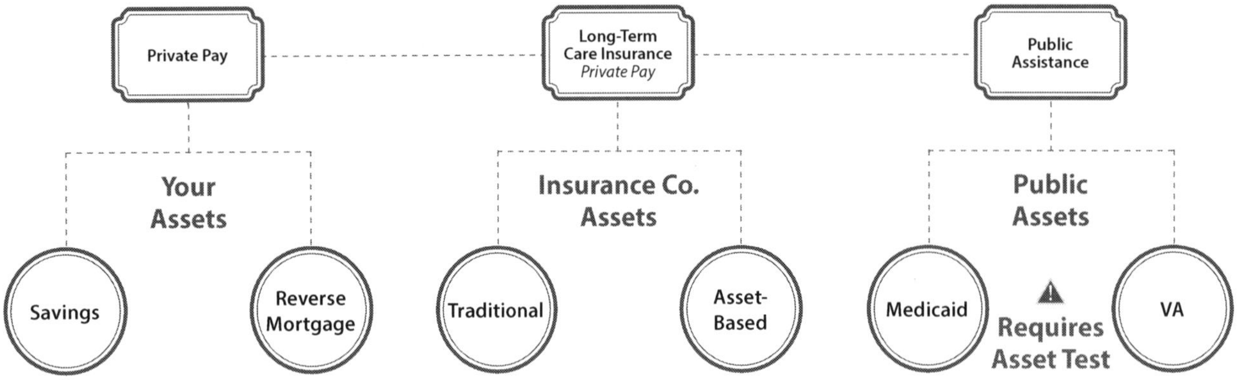

1) Private Pay

There are a variety of ways to pay for long-term care costs. The first is from your own assets.

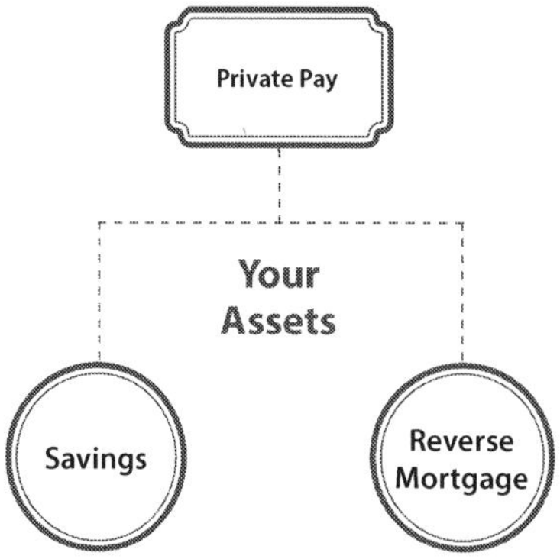

Savings

One of the main reasons people create a retirement nest egg is to have money for medical expenses that occur later in life. While this plan may work for some, for most Americans, it raises a few concerns.

First, long-term care is very expensive. A year or two in a nursing home can use up the savings most Americans acquire over a lifetime.

Another major concern applies to married couples. One person's illness can wipe out the accounts, followed by their death. Then, as the surviving spouse is grieving, they also realize that the rest of their retirement years are now restricted to whatever might be left for them rather than the comfortable plans they originally made. When this surviving spouse becomes ill, now with a reduced nest egg, the result is devastating.

Savings, IRAs, 401ks, 403bs, brokerage, and other accounts can and should be used to help pay for long-term care expenses. However, it can be wise to minimize the risks of this spending by tapping into other means of paying for long-term care costs.

Reverse Mortgage

Reverse mortgages have gotten bad publicity over the years, and they still tend to be one of the most misunderstood financial tools. A reverse mortgage is available to you after the age of 62, and allows you to trade equity in your home for cash. You are not required to pay back the cash as long as you stay in the house. If used correctly and for the right reasons, it can be an effective tool in helping you avoid institutional care.

It is true that past reverse mortgages were guilty of some of the criticism attributed to them, but changes have made them more accessible and the issues that caused hesitation have been corrected.

For example, previously, closing costs could reach tens of thousands of dollars, but thanks to federal regulations, costs are currently capped at $6,000.

Reverse mortgages would also put surviving spouses in the awkward position of having to move and sell the house when their spouse passed away, either because they were not on the original account, they were under 62 years of age, or it was a second marriage. Laws today make it illegal to ask the surviving spouse to move, even if the loan was obtained before the marriage. You will still be asked to move if you fail to pay homeowners insurance or property tax, but that is true of a regular mortgage.

Another thing to take into consideration is that a reverse mortgage is more expensive to establish than a traditional mortgage. Why would you consider a reverse mortgage over a traditional mortgage or line of credit? The answer is that a traditional mortgage always calls for a monthly payment, while a reverse mortgage postpones the payment and makes that amount available to be used to pay for care costs, allowing you to age in your own home.

Who Is the Ideal Candidate for a Reverse Mortgage?

The purpose of reverse mortgages originally was to avoid undesired institutional care. You should only look into reverse mortgages if you have considered every aspect of aging in your own home.

You should be able to afford living in your current home, it must be age-friendly, and you should have the support of a network of loved ones and friends in close proximity. If you are absolutely sure that aging in your current home is the right choice for you and that it is perfectly viable, then a reverse mortgage may be a possibility you should consider.

At that point, you should ask your Financial Planner to include various scenarios of a reverse mortgage in your Financial Dashboard, to see if they improve your outcome. Your Financial Planner may need to consult with a reverse mortgage specialist to ensure the details are input accurately.

How to Best Establish and Use a Reverse Mortgage

Your goal when using a reverse mortgage is to access the equity to pay caregivers, allowing you to age in place. We recommend establishing a line of credit using a reverse mortgage at your earliest opportunity. By doing this, no interest or costs are being incurred (besides the cost to establish the line of credit) because you are not taking out a loan.

The limit for the line of credit — which is how much you can borrow — grows automatically year by year. In fact, the limit grows to accommodate the interest you might have paid, plus an extra 1.25%. A line of credit is also considered a debt and not an asset, meaning it will not interfere with your eligibility for VA benefits or Medicaid.

An alternative to opening a line of credit is taking an amount of the reverse mortgage as a lump sum, or having it paid to you in the form of monthly payments, or a combination of the two. We discourage these options, especially if you are considering VA and Medicaid benefits for long-term care. A lump sum may put your assets over the eligible amount for VA and Medicaid, and you will need to pay that monthly income to the service provider.

If you do decide that a reverse mortgage is a suitable option for you, we encourage you to speak with your family and anyone designated as your caretaker about your decision.

Hiring Caregivers

If you need long-term care, you want the care to come to you, and you don't want your children to become your unpaid caregivers, you will need to hire professionals. This is an expense that needs to be factored into your financial plan.

At the time of this writing (2022), care agencies in the Seattle area charge between $35 and $60 per hour. At these prices, the bill for full-time care can exceed $40,000 a month. Though the hourly rate may be higher or lower in your area, the expense will add up fast no matter where you live.

How can you hire professional caregivers without breaking the bank? Fortunately, working through an agency isn't your only option. Hiring caregivers directly can greatly reduce the cost.

Where do you go to find direct-hire caregivers? The website Care.com is a one option. Most cities also have employment agencies that help families find caregivers for direct hire. In 2022, these caregivers cost under $20 per hour.

If you want your healthcare agent to go the direct hire route, the geriatric care manager you have chosen will play a pivotal role in the caregiver recruitment and selection process. Your geriatric care manager can recruit and interview candidates, choose the best ones, give your healthcare agent a list of candidates to interview personally, and then help make the final selection.

When you go the direct hire route, you can often get round-the-clock in-home care for far less than the cost of care in a nursing home. However, there are downsides. If you hire a caregiver directly, you become the employer, which comes with obligations that you may (or may not) be willing to assume. When you hire caregivers directly, you become responsible for recruiting, interviewing, screening, hiring, training, payroll taxes, workers' compensation, and liability insurance. When the caregiver calls in sick, resigns, or doesn't work out, it's up to you to find a replacement. When you work through an agency, all of these tasks are done for you—but that service comes at a price.

Both options—hiring caregivers directly and working through an agency—have their merits. Be sure to weigh the advantages and disadvantages of each before you make your decision.

Weighing the Options: A Brief Summary

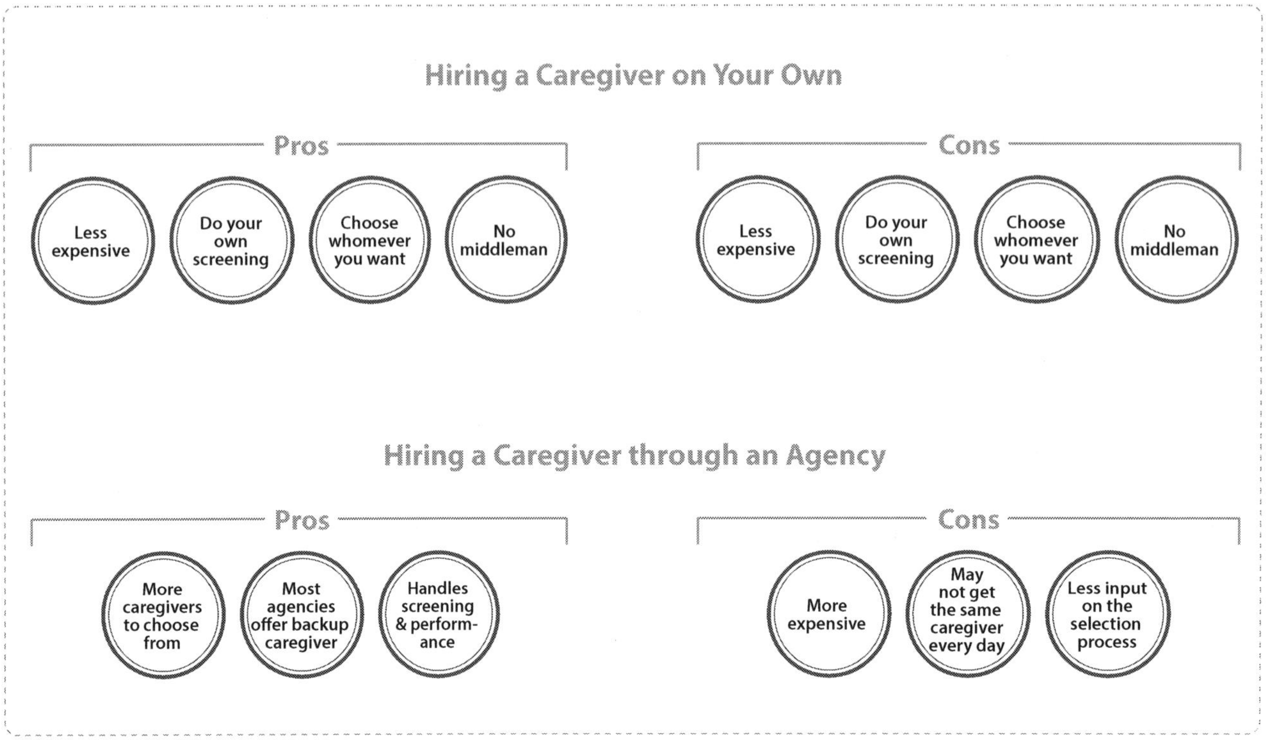

One Family's Experience

We had our Dad's Geriatric Care Manager interview a lot of people and give us three names. We interviewed those people in person. We finally we settled on a couple who came and helped Dad on Monday through Friday. We also hired two older ladies who alternated weekend shifts on Saturday and Sunday. Between these two people, we paid no more than $9,000 in any given month, a lot less than what a nursing home would have cost. Dad was able to continue to live at home, just as he wanted. His health actually improved during the first few years because instead of living alone, he had people living with him and he thrived.

2) Long-Term Care Insurance

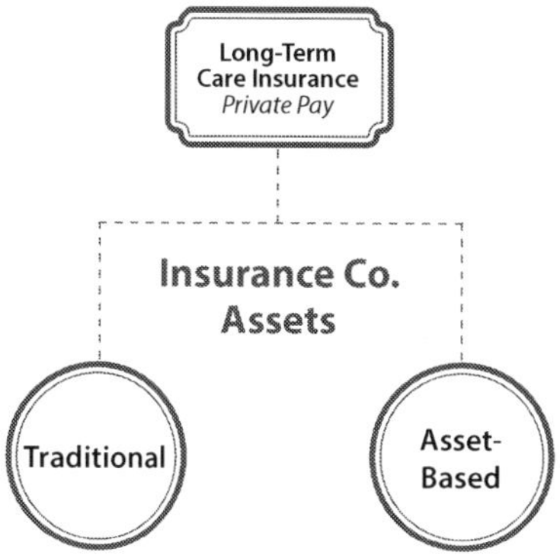

Second, your insurance company assets may include a long-term care (LTC) policy. There are two types of these policies: traditional and asset-based.

Traditional LTC Insurance

The goal of traditional long-term care insurance is to provide the policyholder access to care services then reimburse them the cost of those services. Traditional long-term care insurance policies only pay a benefit when you are no longer able to manage your own activities of daily living (ADL). These ADLs are boiled down to six major tasks: eating, bathing, getting dressed, toileting, transferring, and continence. If you can prove that you are unable to do at least two of these, then the policy will start paying the benefits.

It is suggested that you begin looking for this type of policy around age 50. Premiums for the policy vary based on age, and you should expect to be flexible with terms of the policy and premiums, as premiums will rise over time to account for healthcare cost inflation.

Take note that due to this type of inflation, you may be able to afford the premium between ages 50 and 60, but it may be too expensive to maintain once you reach 65 to 75. Your Financial Dashboard should factor in these rising premiums, and that result will dictate which type of policy is right for you, and whether or not traditional long-term care insurance is right for you at all.

Some may ask: Wouldn't it be smarter to simply save up the premium amount in an account so that it can be accessed when needed, and potentially go to heirs if the need for long-term care never arises? Apart from the practical issue that most people aren't disciplined enough to set aside the money and not touch it, the bigger issue is that you don't know when you might need it. If you haven't saved enough by the time you need access to the money, it would have been better to get the insurance company to foot the bill.

There are other things to note about long-term care policies: There can be a maximum amount paid per day, maximum number of paid days per year, and a lifetime maximum amount. Not all policies have adequate coverage, and policies offer additional benefit for extra fees. Also, certain variables may disqualify you from purchasing a policy, such as poor health or a preexisting diagnosis.

Asset-Based LTC Insurance

If you remain healthy for the rest of your life, and are one of the lucky few who simply never needs long-term care, then the premiums you have paid for traditional long-term care insurance will have had no benefit. If this doesn't sound like an acceptable risk to you, consider asset-based (hybrid) long-term care policies.

These policies start as either annuities or life insurance policies, both of which have death benefits that address the "use it or lose it" concern surrounding traditional policies. Should you simply go to sleep and not wake up, your heirs receive the death benefits so the premiums you pay do not simply vanish into thin air unused.

You determine the amount of money you would like to have to cover future long-term care costs, and the insurance company will present either an annuity or life insurance policy based on the sum. Riders added to the policy allow you to use the benefits as long-term care insurance should the need arise.

These policies tend to be very flexible, allowing various payment plans. Also, because the policies are a fixed benefit, you needn't worry about future premium increases. Asset-based policies are a good option if you are still working and have the disposable income to pay off the policy before retirement or have the funds to pay it off with a single premium.

3) Public Assistance

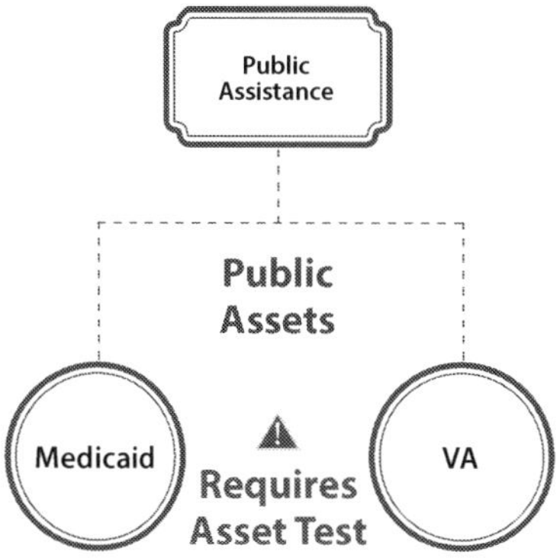

For those whom long-term care policies do not work, a third resource to pay for long-term care costs is via Public Assistance or Public Assets. They are Medicaid and Veterans Affairs (VA) benefits. These two options are only available to those with very limited assets at the time of application. Also, the quality of life provided by these two options is generally poor unless you have other protected assets to supplement the income. Planning to rely on Medicaid or VA without other protected assets is not advisable. Let's look at the two in closer detail.

Medicaid

Medicaid (Government Benefit or Assistance) pays for medical and long-term care costs for those who meet their three requirements: functionality (applicant must functionally or physically need medical or long-term care assistance), income (applicant's income must be insufficient to cover the costs), and resource eligibility (applicant must have spent down their own assets to allowable limits [very low]).

Let's look at each of those requirements individually.

1. The first requirement is that you actually need the assistance of a caregiver, such as in a nursing home, your own home, or another setting. You are automatically approved if you apply while living in a nursing home because your needs are obviously strong enough to require accommodation in that setting. For those not living in a nursing home, we suggest you speak to an Elder Law Attorney knowledgeable in Medicaid requirements because qualifications vary from state to state.

2. Income is the second requirement for Medicaid, and the definition is strict. Referred to as MAGI (Modified Adjusted Gross Income), it is calculated by adding your household's Adjusted Gross Income and tax-exempt interest income together. You should be able to qualify for long-term care under Medicaid as long as your income is below the MAGI threshold (or slightly above to compensate for other medical expenses). It is also still possible to qualify for benefits if your income exceeds the MAGI threshold under what's called the Medically Needy Program.

3. The final requirement for Medicaid eligibility involves your assets, and varies for couples or single people. If you are married, you must only have $2,000 in assets to your name. However, your spouse can have: an unlimited amount of income, a home of any value, an automobile of any value, and other financial assets with specific limitations—and these limitations may be lower than you think. Refer to your Planning Center for updated information.

If you are single, you are still only allowed $2,000 in assets, but you are also allowed to own other assets like a home and a car. In this case, these assets have more limits than the spouse scenario, and the state will put a lien on some properties to recoup some of the cost they are paying toward your care.

The common misconception about Medicaid eligibility is that you and your spouse are not allowed to have any assets to qualify, but that isn't the case. You can legally transfer any amount of your assets to family members, because Medicaid does not look into the assets of other family members and it obviously can't tell you what to do with them.

The only caveat is **the "five-year lookback" rule**. If you gift assets within this period, you may end up making yourself ineligible for Medicaid for some time. With proper planning and preemptive action, your assets can be safely and legally transferred to your beneficiaries, allowing them to use those assets in your best interest while still allowing you to qualify for Medicaid.

VA Benefits

Under the Veterans Affairs (VA) system, there are two programs that may help provide relief to uncovered long-term care costs: VA Compensation Program and the VA Pension Program.

The VA Compensation Program

Available to veterans who have a disability stemming from a wartime injury, and have received an "other than dishonorable" discharge. Since it is an entitlement program as opposed to a means-tested program, it may entitle the veteran to a disability payment that is not dependent on that veteran's income or assets.

Veterans who have become incapacitated to the point that they need assistance from others, either in a home or institutional care setting, may be eligible for additional benefits. The reason behind the need for care must be directly tied to a wartime injury, which is the same with the Dependents Indemnity Compensation program. This program provides the widower or widow of the veteran with the continued disability benefits should the veteran die of wartime-related injuries.

VA Pension Program

The VA Pension Program is also called the "Housebound" or the "Aid and Attendance" program. This is another disability program, however it does not require the veteran to have suffered a wartime injury like the VA Compensation Program does. Instead, the program qualifies veterans based on their means. In order to qualify, the veteran must show that their medical costs require them to pay so much out of their household income that what's left is below the threshold that the VA has established as too low. Eligible veterans who require aid may be eligible for extra monetary assistance for their care needs.

There are three elements that determine your eligibility for Pension Program benefits: your Veteran Status, an Income Test, and an Asset Test. Generally, if you served 90 days in active duty and at least one of those days was during a declared wartime, you may qualify as an eligible veteran. The income and asset tests are very similar to those of the Medicaid program.

Planning for Medicaid & VA Eligibility

As you put together a strategy for your future that may include Medicaid and/or VA benefits, it is very important to include a plan around tax issues. One that can sneak up on you is your IRA. If you fall ill and need to move your assets to your spouse to qualify for public benefits, one of the most expensive to transfer is your Traditional IRA. ***Transferring this account can cost twenty percent or more.***

However, there is something you can do to mitigate this cost—

Convert your IRA to a Roth IRA

Because of the tax costs on transfers of a Traditional account, Roth accounts would be highly beneficial to you if you ever need to apply for Medicaid or VA programs. Roth IRA accounts are tax-free for future withdrawals, an invaluable boon to you should you need to liquidate a large amount of assets before applying for Medicaid and VA programs.

If you have a Traditional Retirement account, you can convert part or all of it to a Roth account anytime. There are no amount or age limits to this conversion. The catch? The amount that you convert does get taxed as income that year.

Why would you pay taxes now to avoid paying the same taxes later? The key reason is tax brackets. The higher your income, the higher the percentage in taxes you must pay. The advantage to converting to a Roth account is that you can decide how much to convert, and you can do part of the account each year. That way, you pay less in total taxes, and over a longer time, than suddenly getting a large tax bill in the middle of a health crisis when needing Medicaid or VA benefits.

The Roth account gives you flexibility. Most Financial Planners consider only the marginal tax savings of a Roth Conversion strategy, and therefore may not recommend it. But with this additional information, you can insist on thoroughly considering the wisdom of adding future flexibility to your financial plan by converting your Traditional retirement accounts to Roth over time.

Now that you have some ideas about what questions to ask, it's time to obtain a thorough Financial Dashboard report from your Financial Planner. With their software, expertise, and your new knowledge of what questions you need answered, you can confidently make your decisions.

Financial: Address Long-Term Care Costs

Answer this section after reviewing a thorough Financial Dashboard with your Financial Planner.

Long-Term Care: Private Pay Solutions:

- ☐ I plan to utilize Private Pay for Long-Term Care
  - ☐ I will draw from my savings
  - ☐ I will use a reverse mortgage
  - ☐ I'm ready to speak with a Reverse Mortgage Specialist
  - ☐ I will establish a path so my agents can hire caregivers directly or through an agency

Long-Term Care: Insurance Solutions:

- ☐ I plan to use Long-Term Care Insurance
  - ☐ I will use a Traditional Plan
  - ☐ I will use an Asset-Based Plan
  - ☐ I'm ready to speak with a Long-Term Care Insurance Agent

Long-Term Care: Public Assistance Solutions:

- ☐ I plan to use Public Assistance
  - ☐ I will apply for Medicaid
  - ☐ I will apply for VA Benefits
  - ☐ I'm ready to speak with an Elder Law Attorney for help qualifying for benefits

Notes regarding my plan to cover Long-Term Care Costs:

____

____

____

Minimize Your Financial Burden on Others

Most of us hope to avoid becoming a burden on our loved ones. But without adequate planning, you are almost assured that you will become exactly that. Luckily, with a bit of planning you can greatly relieve the burden you will place on loved ones.

Why does this happen? Traditional documents assume that your fiduciary will simply "figure it out" when the time comes. The fiduciary is essentially expected to act on your behalf without much direction, making even the simplest tasks a challenge and a hardship.

How can you prevent this from happening? For better outcomes, you will want to meet and consult with your fiduciaries to make your wishes very clear and specific. You will also want to come up with a very detailed and specific outline for your fiduciary, ensuring that they have sufficient guidance and resources to act on your behalf when you cannot.

Financial tasks that are expected of your fiduciary fall under three broad categories:

- Paying bills
- Filing taxes
- Managing your financial holdings such as investments or properties

Additional tasks

- Arranging a go-to healthcare professional prepared to coordinate your care the way you want is an incredibly important step
- You will also need to consider and coordinate their access to your personal information

Let's discuss ways to lighten the burden for your fiduciaries.

Acquire a Financial Planner

You are likely leaving financial assets in the hands of your fiduciaries. Arranging to have a Financial Planner not only protects you and your assets, it gives your fiduciaries a reliable source of knowledge and advice to lean on for help. Make sure that the Financial Planner you choose to oversee your documents and assist your fiduciaries is someone you trust and have had experience with in the past. You should also make sure that this planner has a succession plan that you are comfortable with in case they retire or go out of business. You will want to name this person as the professional you want your fiduciaries to work with.

Arrange for a Property Manager

If you have rental properties, consider hiring a property manager. Not everyone is comfortable with managing properties, and your fiduciary may not be interested in managing a property they have no connection to. Having a manager deal with your properties can alleviate a major and undue burden to your loved ones. Consider delegating tasks to potential property managers to build a relationship and figure out whether or not they are right for the job. Once you identify someone, be sure to name them in your documents.

Set Up Bill Pay

More than likely the first financial task your fiduciary will have to deal with is paying your bills. Without guidance, figuring out what bills need to be paid, to whom, when, and how much, is one of the biggest challenges your fiduciary will face.

One option to reduce this burden is to use software your fiduciary can access to track and pay your bills. Banks offer this service, but if you or your fiduciary chooses to change banks, you will lose your electronic history.

Alternatively, you can use a program not attached to any single institution. There are several programs you can use, including QuickBooks™, Quicken®, and Mvelops®, among others. These programs are a way to track income, expenses, deductions, and other financial histories. If you choose to use a program to track your bills, it would be wise to make sure that your fiduciary becomes familiar with the program to ensure ease of use in the future.

If you want to eliminate the burden altogether, consider arranging for an accountant or bookkeeper to take over the role of bill payer and assist your fiduciary when the time comes. Ask your current accountant if they can help your fiduciary in this role. If they don't, consider finding an accountant who does. When you have found an accountant you are comfortable with, you will want to name that accountant in your Powers of Attorney documents so your fiduciary knows whom to contact.

Hire an Accountant for Taxes

Filing your taxes is another financial issue that your fiduciary may struggle with. Filing taxes are hard at the best of times—having to file someone else's taxes without any guidance or knowledge of their finances is an extreme burden. Consider hiring a local accountant to manage your taxes, and build a professional relationship, trust, and history, as opposed to a tax preparation factory. By having a history and trust with this accountant, you can be confident that your fiduciaries will receive competent and reliable services when it comes to preparing your taxes.

You should also make sure that your accountant has competent and trustworthy people who can take over your account if your accountant retires or leaves the business.

If you do not wish to hire an accountant to prepare your taxes in the event that you can no longer handle your affairs, we suggest that you sit down with your fiduciaries and do your taxes a few years in a row so that they are familiar with your process and financial situation.

Password Management

You will want to provide a list of log-in credentials, passwords and account information your fiduciaries may need to be able to manage your accounts electronically.

A word of caution: for most sites it is illegal to impersonate a real user—meaning that others should not log into the system using your ID and conduct business as if they were you. Although there are a few ways for them to be able to quickly and easily manage your affairs without your credentials, it is extremely difficult to give them authority over your accounts equal to yourself. Proceed with this recommendation with caution, and make sure that your agents know that they cannot access your accounts and impersonate you.

Prepay Funeral Expenses

When it comes to funeral expenses, consider prepaying final expenses and being clear about funerary decisions. By prepaying your final expenses, you not only save money, you save your loved ones the burden of having to think about it and pay for it themselves later.

You should also decide and be clear about what to do with your remains. If you decide you want to be cremated, what do you want your loved ones to do with your ashes?

- Do you want them interred in a columbarium?
- Scattered in the ocean?
- Used to nourish plants and trees?
- Made into jewelry?
- Shot into space?

By making these decisions well beforehand and offering your fiduciaries and loved ones a clear and specific guide, you are saving them time, money, and alleviating burdens that would otherwise befall them in a very emotional and difficult time of their lives.

By the way, under current Medicaid rules, prepaid funeral and burial costs are not counted as part of your estate, so you will not only be helping to prevent a burden on your fiduciaries, you can plan for Medicaid at the same time should you need it.

Veterans can also receive aid under the VA burial benefits, but costs related to handling remains are not covered, so consider prepaying these expenses.

Select a Geriatric Care Manager

Naming a Geriatric Care Manager in your instruction manual is crucial.

Here's why: If you fall and end up in the hospital, and the nurse asks your Power of Attorney which rehab center to send you to, what do you want them to say?

Hopefully, by now, you realize that you can give them the tools to bring you home, if at all possible. But the nurse isn't able to authorize that on the word of your Power of Attorney alone—and that's where the Geriatric Care Manager comes in. This designated person will establish and obtain the equipment and support you need for care in your home. By pre-interviewing and selecting a Geriatric Care Manager, and then writing them into your documents, your Power of Attorney is empowered to call them at this critical moment. He or she can come in, talk to the nurse and doctors, outline an agreeable plan of care, and you wake up in your own home, just as you planned.

Take a moment to identify the professionals that you should include in your financial team.

When it comes to the financial plan, and especially the Dashboard, we strongly recommend that you work with a competent Financial Planner. The combination of sophisticated software, experience, and training are worth the time and effort you put into finding a competent and trusted planner.

Of all the professionals to assemble on your team, a critical one who is often overlooked is the Geriatric Care Manager. This person will be the quarterback for your care needs if you fall ill, and will be a keystone to relieving those burdens from your loved ones.

Financial: Minimize Burden on Others

I plan to minimize burdens on others by doing the following: (Select all that apply)

- ☐ Acquire a Financial Planner – and name them in my Agent Instructions with my Powers of Attorney
- ☐ Acquire an Accountant for Taxes – and name them in my Agent Instructions with my Powers of Attorney
- ☐ Set up Bill Pay – and detail my system for my Agents
- ☐ Set up Password Management – and make the list easily accessible to my Agents
- ☐ Prepay Final Expenses – and make the forms easily accessible to my Agents
- ☐ Acquire a Property Manager or Handyman – and name them in my Agent Instructions with my Powers of Attorney
- ☐ Arrange for a Geriatric Care Manager – and name them in my Agent Instructions with my Powers of Attorney

Notes regarding my plan to minimize my burden on others:

Legal Planning

For Your Retirement

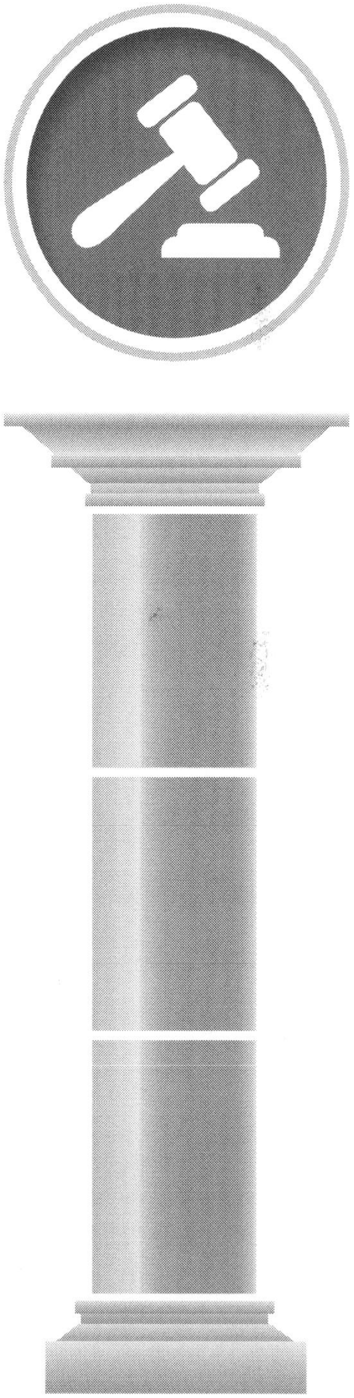

As you map out your *LifePlan* in the other areas, making Housing, Health, and Financial plans, these plans need to be protected. That is where Legal plans come in. For example, the best laid plan for your future housing could be wiped out when a spouse falls ill or passes away without the proper legal documents in place.

To whatever degree you have or have not put together estate planning legal documents, you hope to achieve certain goals for your future and your family's future. Unfortunately, even if you have binders of documents, it may not be the right recipe to ensure that you achieve your goals. The entirety of traditional estate planning is made up of a handful of legal documents: a Will or Trust, Powers of Attorney, and a Living Will. Yes… these documents are important, and everyone planning their retirement needs them. They address the three major issues of estate planning:

1. ***Who gets what from your estate when you die***
2. ***Who has the legal authority to manage your affairs until you die***
3. ***Whether or not you want artificial life support; or in other words, how you'd like to die***

Well, with that plan, ***congratulations!*** You are ready to die!

If you think about it, who is really using these documents? We'll give you a hint—*it's not you*. It will be your loved ones, who must step in and carry out your wishes when you cannot. Will they know what to do?

Relying solely on the usual verbiage found in these documents for your retirement planning can leave dangerous gaps in the security of your plan. An important step when implementing a *LifePlan* is to work with a qualified attorney who can draft these documents with you and your family in mind. Since your family will be the ones using them, these documents ought to read like **Manuals of Instruction**. And, to accomplish that, you first need to know what instructions you want to provide.

LifePlanning is designed to empower you to focus on the quality of the life you have remaining. Creating and implementing your comprehensive *LifePlan* is a way to ensure that you achieve your retirement goals.

Let's get started.

Protect Your Assets

As we saw in the Financial pillar, the major issue that can torpedo your financial future is a long-term care need. When we talk about protecting assets, we are referring to the goal of not running out of money. The root reason that people have this goal is to preserve their quality of life, and this should be true even after one's health deteriorates. By protecting assets, you can be more assured that your wishes and goals will be achieved throughout your life.

Here is an example from Rajiv Nagaich:

Early in my career, I helped a family whose mother was in a nursing home and they were looking to protect her remaining assets from being lost to Medicaid and to the nursing home.

A year or so later, I decided to visit their mother. I was shocked and angered to find that she was living in the same room and her quality of life had not improved one bit. Upset by the thought that maybe our work was simply ensuring that the children would obtain an inheritance, I called the family to inquire how the funds we saved them were being used. Unfortunately, they knew the funds would be used for expenses that came up, but it never occurred to them that the funds could improve their mother's day-to-day life. With a little guidance and help from a care manager, their mother could have achieved a higher quality of life.

This family wasn't malicious; they were simply uninformed. It is important that a knowledgeable Elder Law Attorney does not simply know how to protect assets, but also knows how to guide the use of those assets to improve the life of the individual.

*The first legal tool to understand is a special type of Trust called a **Safe Harbor Trust.***

A Safe Harbor Trust is a specific and customized variation of a Special Needs Trust.

Safe Harbor Trusts can be customized to offer protection against more than just asset loss or long-term care costs. As you age, you will need to address financial, legal, and housing issues related to being incapacitated. You will also want to plan for protection against scam artists taking advantage of the elderly.

Let's take a look at how a Safe Harbor Trust can be used in each of these scenarios.

Uncovered Long-Term Care Costs

The most significant financial threat facing the average American today is suffering a serious illness...without any healthcare coverage. The problem is, if there is no cure for what you are suffering from, or if you need the help of others to manage your day-to-day living, your care will not be covered in any meaningful way by Medicare or other health insurance policies. And for most Americans, the question isn't whether or not they will have to deal with these unexpected costs—the question is when.

An important tool to have at the ready for this scenario is in the protective provisions of a Safe Harbor Trust. The Trust protects assets from being exhausted before a person can qualify for medical and long-term care benefits from Medicaid and the VA systems.

Congress passed a law after recognizing that individuals with small-to-medium estates need to be able to access long-term care without spending down all of their assets. This law acknowledges that without any assets to supplement benefits provided by Medicaid and the VA, individuals will have a poorer quality of life.

You have options when planning to protect yourself from long-term care costs:

- You can buy a long-term care insurance policy, which we discussed in the Financial section, but this may not be an option due to the cost of these policies.
- Another option is to plan around Medicaid and/or VA benefits, but this requires strategic planning and is generally only helpful to those with little to no assets.

Because of these reasons, those with small-to-medium size estates can benefit immensely from the protection offered by a Safe Harbor Trust, especially when it comes to uncovered long-term care costs.

Medicaid and VA Benefits

There are some things to know about VA and Medicaid benefits.

As we learned in the Financial section, both the VA and Medicaid have programs designed to cover long-term care costs. However, these programs are generally available to individuals with very low asset balances, in addition to the other eligibility rules.

The rules behind qualifying for Medicaid and what benefits you receive under that program are different from those of the VA program. Medicaid is considered the more generous of the two.

Under VA benefits, you are also required to use your own household income to cover care costs, which could leave your living spouse without a means of support. There will only be a limited amount to help cover the gap between your care costs and your household income.

In most instances, the steps required to qualify for Medicaid may disqualify you from VA benefits, and vice versa. In some cases, however, it is helpful to qualify for both (if you are able), so it may be in your best interest to speak with an Elder Law Attorney who is knowledgeable about both programs before you make any decisions.

It is also important to recognize that Medicaid is usually more generous with married couples than single applicants. Once a spouse passes away, the living spouse is then considered single, making it important for you to plan ahead and know the rules for both types of application.

Subsequent Marriages

Sometimes it's hard to imagine your spouse being in subsequent relationships after your passing. In these cases, leaving your assets to your spouse in order to provide support after your passing seems like the best route to protect your loved one. This is done under the assumption that the remaining assets will be distributed to heirs that you and your spouse have agreed upon.

What happens when your surviving spouse lives on longer than anticipated? The need for human companionship doesn't necessarily go away. It isn't surprising or uncommon when the surviving spouse enters a new relationship. This is true even if the surviving parent has strong ties with the children. The children have their own families, and the surviving parent feels as if they shouldn't bother their children.

The problem comes when this need for companionship is filled by a person who may take advantage of your surviving spouse when they are at their most vulnerable. For example, they could pressure your spouse into listing them as the beneficiary or heir and removing other heirs. Or, simply gain access to assets for themselves, and deplete funds that were intended for your spouse's needs.

Protection for your spouse and their assets can come in the form of a Prenuptial Agreement or a Property Status Agreement, but these are not the most effective since most couples forgo Prenuptial Agreements due to awkward negotiations and the fact that they only protect assets from a subsequent divorce.

While this is better than no protection, a Safe Harbor Trust is still your best bet as it will put any assets you've left to your surviving spouse out of reach of anyone trying to manipulate them, while at the same time remaining available to your surviving spouse and your intended heirs.

Estate Tax

Another protection commonly found in a Trust is from Estate Taxes. This is a consideration when the scenario is at the opposite end of the financial spectrum, and you may find yourself with a few million dollars or more in estate value. The IRS, and some states, will impose a tax on estates above this range. This is called an Estate Tax.

To reduce this tax, the Safe Harbor Trust can include legal language that sets aside half of the estate when the first spouse dies, keeping the taxable estate below the threshold of estate taxes. This can help to maintain your legacy, and reduce the burden on your loved ones from having to sell off businesses or real estate to pay an estate tax after you've passed away.

Protecting Inheritances

If there is a possibility that you would be receiving an inheritance at some point, it should be considered in your *LifePlanning* process.

Specifically, you may want to have this inheritance directed to a Safe Harbor Trust with you as the beneficiary and a trusted person as the trustee. This is to avoid having the inheritance added to your estate, which may disqualify you for Medicaid.

Thought should also be put into protecting your children's inheritance. This inheritance can be at risk of being vulnerable to creditors, divorcing spouses, and financial mismanagement. An Inheritance Protection Trust (a type of Safe Harbor Trust) can be used in many cases to protect your children's inheritance from themselves and others.

The idea behind an Inheritance Protection Trust is that instead of leaving your assets directly to your heir, you instead leave it to a Trust. When you pass, your assets are put into the Trust with your child as the beneficiary and a trusted individual as a co-trustee. Your child will not be able to take money out of the trust without the approval of your co-trustee. For more information on Inheritance Protection Trusts, talk to a knowledgeable Elder Law Attorney.

Types of Trusts

As you work with your Estate Planning Attorney to determine whether a Safe Harbor Trust is the right option for you—and which provisions to add to it—you should also understand that there are two ways to enact it: ***Now*** and ***Later***.

Now - Inter Vivos Trust (often used by single people)

This form of Trust is most commonly used by someone who is unmarried, and is known as a Stand-Alone Safe Harbor Trust, or an Inter Vivos Safe Harbor Trust. This is actually the only option available if you are single, but it is also an option for couples when they want to immediately place assets into a Safe Harbor Trust.

Caution must be taken before using an Inter Vivos Trust, however, because transfer of assets is not revocable. Plus, assets put into this Trust are subject to the Medicaid five-year lookback.

For a more in-depth look at the specific planning process for these types of Safe Harbor Trusts, please speak with a knowledgeable Elder Law Attorney.

Later - Testamentary Trust (often used by couples)

More frequently utilized by married couples is the Testamentary Safe Harbor Trust. It is essentially a blueprint for a Trust, and it is created inside of your Will but not activated until after the first spouse's passing.

You are not required to put your assets into the Trust when you create it. What does this mean? It means nothing changes in your life, and you retain all your assets until your death, as well as the ability to change your mind as long as you remain mentally competent. After you pass, your surviving spouse decides which half of the estate is moved into the Safe Harbor Trust. It is at that point that the protections of the Trust become activated.

Married couples can use this legal planning tool to effectively protect their spouse from problems with Medicaid, subsequent spouses, or estate taxes.

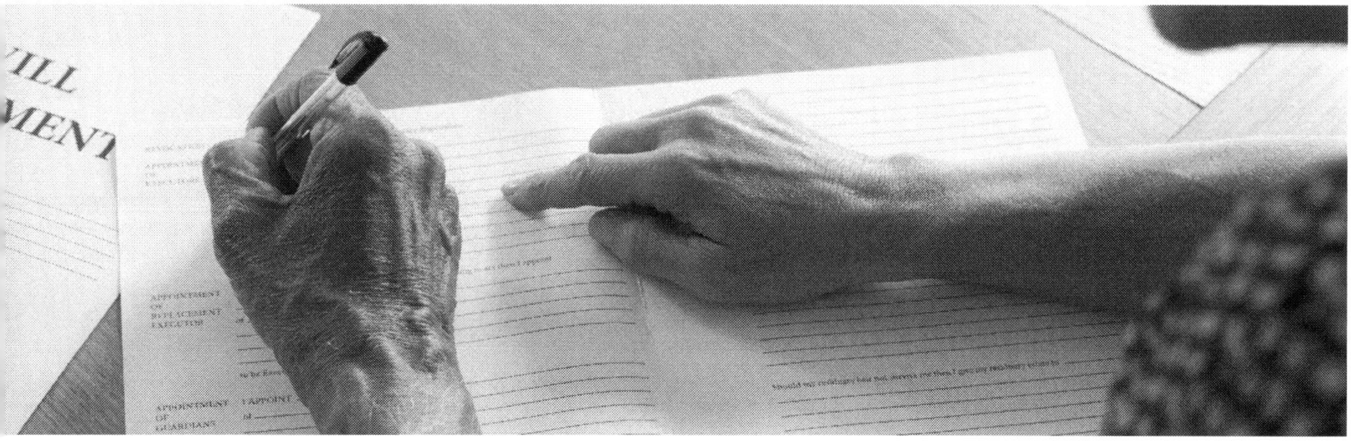

If you end up instituting a Safe Harbor Trust for the purpose of an inheritance—whether for your heirs or someone instituting one for you—it will be in the form of the Testamentary Safe Harbor Trust. Remember, this means it exists as a clause inside another Trust or Will and becomes a full-fledged Trust with all its protections when that person passes away.

It's wise to consult with an Elder Law or Estate Planning Attorney familiar with these strategies.

Align Beneficiaries

If you decide to incorporate the protections of a Safe Harbor Trust to protect your assets, be sure that you change your beneficiary designations on things such as your life insurance policies, bank accounts, annuities, financial holdings, etc. to align with your planning around the Safe Harbor Trust in your Will or Trust. This is because the designations in your other financial documents generally outweigh your Will or Trust, meaning that if you do not change your beneficiary designations in your other documents, your wishes may not be realized.

Let's Pause to Plan: On the subsequent pages, make notes about what you would like to focus on with this topic, or cross out anything that you know does not apply to you.

Legal: Protect Assets (Trust Protections)

I am interested in utilizing a Trust to protect my assets from the following threats:

(Select all that apply)

- ☐ Uncovered Long-Term Care Costs
- ☐ Subsequent Marriages
- ☐ Estate Taxes
- ☐ Inheritance risks

I would like to meet with an Elder Law Attorney to learn which trusts are best for me:

- ☐ Yes
- ☐ Not yet
- ☐ Undecided

Notes regarding my plan to protect my assets:

I plan to consult with my Attorney to align the following beneficiary designations:

(Select all that apply)

- ☐ Bank Accounts
- ☐ Brokerage Accounts (stocks, bonds, mutual funds, etc.)
- ☐ Retirement Accounts (IRA, 401(k), etc.)
- ☐ Life Insurance (annuities, etc.)
- ☐ Real Estate (houses, property, time shares, etc.)
- ☐ Business Ownership (Sole Proprietorship, LLC, Partnerships, etc.)
- ☐ Other

Minimize Burden on Others

The second theme in the Legal pillar is Minimizing Burdens on loved ones. There are several key ways to achieve that goal. Among them are:

1. **Finalizing your Estate Plans**
2. **Selecting your Fiduciaries**
3. **Creating Manuals of Instruction**

Finalize Estate Planning

Beyond Wills and Trusts, there are a host of additional legal documents that are equally significant when planning for your future, including Powers of Attorney, Advance Care Directives and others. Let's learn about the most significant documents to include in your estate plan.

Durable Healthcare Power of Attorney

The person you appoint with this power will make healthcare decisions for you when you are unable to do that yourself. Whether that is due to a coma, dementia, or other illness, when you are incapacitated it is critical to allow someone close to you to manage these choices.

Durable Financial Power of Attorney

As you might guess, this appoints someone the power to act in your stead in matters of banking, taxes, finances, and similar areas. If you are sick, who will pay the bills? Your Power of Attorney for Finances, that's who.

You may have noticed that both of these Powers of Attorney started with the word "Durable." This means that, although you sign the documents while you are well, they have effect even when you are ill, too.

Mental Health Advance Directive

This gives your agent the ability to seek mental health treatment and/or evaluation for you against your objections. While this may sound undesirable, it can make the difference when you yourself are on the cognitive decline and can no longer identify that you need mental help, which is a frequently overlooked issue. Make sure you have discussions with your agents before including this provision, as it can be misused by someone with malicious intent.

Living Will

This provides guidance to your named agents about your wishes in terms of being kept alive by external means. The matter can be more complicated than it sounds, since there are many variables that go into not only your agent's forming their decision, but whether or not their decision matters.

For example, in Texas, if the medical community deems that life support is futile and you will never get better, then it doesn't matter what your agents decide; you will not be given life support.

Since there are different scenarios regarding how and when these Living Wills come into effect, the most important things to keep in mind are: 1) who is your agent, and 2) what are the laws governing life support in your state.

It may also benefit you to understand how a Living Will works in the practical world, not just the legal world, so looking at some high-profile cases on the subject (such as the Terri Schiavo case) may serve to help you make better-informed decisions.

For more information on laws surrounding the subject, speak to a knowledgeable Elder Law Attorney.

POLST: Because Living Wills have no standard, normalized form, it is difficult for medical professionals to quickly review them during a crisis situation. The Physician's Order on Life Sustaining Treatment (POLST) was created to address this issue and to let any and all healthcare providers know your wishes.

There are some aspects of the POLST to be cautious about, however. Considered a doctor's order, a POLST must be carried out by everyone in the healthcare community, even if the attending physician is unavailable for consultation, which could lead to disastrous results. Because of this, it is worth knowing how a POLST form works, how it can benefit you, how it can negatively affect you, and what to do with your POLST form when you are no longer in a healthcare setting.

Recommendation: While planning your legal affairs, it is typically wiser to rely on a Living Will than a POLST form.

Handling of Remains

The document used to outline your preferences on how you want your remains to be handled—burial, cremation, or another option—may be called Directive for Handling My Remains, Directive of Disposition of Remains, or Disposition Authorization. No matter the name, the document is used to outline your preferences on how you want your remains to be handled, whether it be by burial, cremation, or another option.

Why is this important? In the Financial section, we discussed how prepaying your final expenses helps reduce the financial burden on your loved ones. Creating a legal Handling of Remains document completes the process of easing the burden of your passing. Not only will it clearly express your specific wishes at a stressful time, it will also help prevent disagreements between your family members who may have differing opinions. This step is a precious gift that you can give to those you leave behind.

At this point, pause to consider this topic and make notes about what you'd like to focus on, or cross out anything that you know doesn't apply to you.

Legal: Minimize burdens

I plan to minimize burdens on others by acquiring the following: (Select all that apply)

- ☐ Healthcare Power of Attorney
- ☐ Financial Power of Attorney
- ☐ Mental Health Advance Directive
- ☐ Living Will (Advance Directive)
- ☐ Handling of Remains

I would like to meet with an Elder Law/Estate Planning Attorney to help me create my estate planning documents:

- ☐ Yes
- ☐ No
- ☐ Undecided

Notes regarding my plan to minimize burdens:

Choose Fiduciaries

You've probably noted that most of the legal documents for estate planning require you to name someone who will act on your behalf. Any of these roles—whether a Trustee of a Trust or a Power of Attorney—is generally referred to as a Fiduciary.

Choosing your fiduciaries can be one of the most important and delicate aspects of planning. Your fiduciaries will be legally empowered to act on your behalf when you are no longer able to do so, both in life and death. Because of this, it is of the utmost importance that you choose fiduciaries that you trust completely, and that you communicate your wishes with them clearly.

Loved Ones as Fiduciaries

One of the core concepts behind *LifePlanning* is to realize that aging is a family affair. This is particularly obvious when selecting family as your fiduciaries.

Retirement planning should be more than just getting your affairs in order before you pass. Planning can provide peace of mind to your loved ones. When they are included in your planning process, it can serve to help them come to terms with your death or illness.

When considering family members as your fiduciaries, keep in mind that we all age. For that reason, those who are of a similar age will also age along with you and may not be much more capable than you when the time comes to step in and act. For this reason, it is common to look to children or younger generation loved ones as fiduciaries. However, many professionals discourage selecting co-fiduciaries to avoid disruption to your estate and beneficiaries during an emotional time.

While your children may benefit from being named your fiduciaries, it can also be a burden. To help alleviate this burden, we recommend that you prioritize having family conversations so that your wishes are clear and detailed and everyone in the family knows their role and what is expected of them. By having these discussions, you can help minimize the chances of your family arguing when a crisis hits. The chapter on Family Planning will go over this in detail.

Professional Fiduciaries

In some scenarios it may be best to seek someone outside of your family or network of loved ones to be your fiduciary. Selecting a professional as your fiduciary can be a viable option. A professional fiduciary agent appointed as your Power of Attorney or Trustee will charge for their time. This can be a mutually beneficial arrangement, but on average it does cost more than a paid family member.

You can also authorize a law firm or other trusted professional advisor with whom you have a relationship to elect a professional fiduciary for you. Generally, many advisors are familiar with what is required of agents under Powers of Attorney and some offer fiduciary services themselves. You should know, however, that going this route may cause some conflict of interest with whatever advisor is electing your professional fiduciary.

You could also locate a professional fiduciary yourself. They undergo some training and can be found on court-created registries. However, consider the wisdom of letting the court elect your fiduciary. Not all of these professionals are the same, and it will benefit you immensely if you meet with these individuals until you find and build a relationship with the one you know you can trust. Only then should you start preparing your estate documents with this professional named as your fiduciary.

NOTE: While it will cause a degree of burden on your loved ones, there is also evidence that going through the process of serving as your fiduciary in your time of need is a learning moment. The process, whether it's a smaller burden from your good planning or a heavy burden without it, often inspires them to complete their own planning, which can help their own future.

By going through the process of *LifePlanning*, you can reduce the burden on them, but taking it away completely may also rob them of a milestone in their own experience. For these reasons, a professional fiduciary may be the way to go when you do not have a loved one who could take on the responsibility.

For some, choosing fiduciaries is simple, but for others it can be a complicated decision.

Take time to ponder and discuss, and write down your notes here.

Legal: Choose Fiduciaries

When selecting fiduciaries: (Select all that apply)

- ☐ I plan to select family/loved ones as my fiduciaries
- ☐ I plan to select Professional fiduciaries
- ☐ I plan to name Co-Fiduciaries

Notes regarding my Fiduciary Plans:

Manuals of Instruction

Now that we have covered the documents you'll encounter and how to think through whom to name as fiduciaries, let's connect these at a level deeper than traditional planning.

This is a critical topic to request of your Estate Planning or Elder Law Attorney. In order to minimize the burden that assigning the role of fiduciary creates, a manual of instruction is needed—and it should come from you! This can be written and codified right into your legal documents.

Let's take a look at some key areas to map out.

Care Management Provisions

When you become incapacitated, your agents will step in to handle your care, whether that means caring for you themselves or establishing care by someone else. The problem is… it is likely that your agent will have neither the skills nor the know-how to ensure you are cared for properly.

To this end, you should think about including provisions in your Power of Attorney and Safe Harbor Trust that guide your agents toward hiring the aid of a Geriatric Care Manager. This trained person will be able to assess your situation and guide your agents in providing proper care.

This role is covered in the Financial chapter as well. Here we emphasize that you can direct your fiduciary to call a specific Geriatric Care Manager if you fall ill, and name them right in your legal documents.

Bar against Guardianship

Even though one of the main reasons to draft your Power of Attorney is to have a say in who provides your care, sadly it may not always be the case. Guardianship proceedings (where the court becomes involved in who handles your affairs) may be forced on your agents by disgruntled relatives or professional services who cite your best interests but, in reality, are looking out for themselves. You can include provisions in your Power of Attorney that make it very clear you trust your named agents over outsiders.

Prohibitions

Your Power of Attorney can include provisions that prohibit your agents from signing voluntary arbitration agreements. Arbitration agreements are documents that forfeit your right to sue a housing facility in situations of negligence or inaction that lead to your injury. By including provisions with specific instructions for this situation, any arbitration agreement your agents may sign to get you accepted into a facility become invalid. Your agent can still sign the entrance application like normal, but if a situation should arise later that necessitates litigation, this provision would allow you and your agent more options to fight for your rights.

Professional Resources

One of the main failings of a traditional Power of Attorney document is that while it is intended to ease the burden on your loved ones, in most cases it lacks the guidance to follow through on that benefit.

You can, and should, include in your Power of Attorney provisions and specific, detailed guidance as to whom your agents should work with when dealing with your affairs. This can include the following professionals and services:

- A Geriatric Care Manager
- Your Financial Planner
- An accountant or bookkeeper to aid with taxes or bills
- A property manager
- A specific Geriatrician
- Your online banking accesses
- Your funeral arrangements, which we strongly encourage you to prepay

By doing this, you take away much of the legwork that your agents need to do to carry out your wishes and provide you with the care you both need and want.

Your list should also include backup professionals. Remember that your agents may not use this list until many years from now. What if one of the professionals on the list has retired or gone out of business? It's a good idea to include one or two backups for each category.

Compensation

Ensure that your agents and loved ones are fairly compensated for their time and effort. It can be disastrous to assume that they do not expect any compensation because of your relationship. While this may be true at first, by not compensating them you will more than likely burden them financially, socially, physically, mentally, etc. Do not take your agents and loved ones for granted; ensure that they are properly compensated.

A good starting point is to understand what a professional fiduciary would cost. You do not need to provide the same level of compensation, particularly since a loved one is not likely a professional in this area, but this helps give you one way to start thinking of what this amount might be.

Alternatively, in some families there is a home that might make sense to gift in its entirety to the fiduciary, while the rest of the heirs split everything else. There are several ways to accomplish this, so work through your unique circumstances with an Estate Planning or Elder Law Attorney.

Legal: Manuals of Instruction

I plan to include the following provisions for my Fiduciaries: (Select all that apply)

- ☐ Care Management
- ☐ Prohibitions
- ☐ Bar against Guardianship
- ☐ Professional Resources
- ☐ Compensation

Notes regarding my plan to create Manuals of Instruction:

Review Your Legal Plan

We have covered several important concepts in the realm of legal estate documents. We certainly don't intend for you to draft these yourself; you will need to work with a competent legal counsel who can advise you and create these for you. But as you've been reading, learning, and taking notes, you should now feel more confident—knowing what you'll want an attorney to provide. So, instead of feeling lost or reliant on a professional (without knowing whether their approach is best for you), you can now walk into the attorney's office with a list of your preferences and know just where to start.

Legal documents within an AgingOptions *LifePlan* will protect your wishes, ensuring that your decisions are legally protected and your fiduciaries are legally empowered to carry out those wishes.

Look at the AgingOptions Resource Guide to find Elder Law Attorneys near you who can help draft your legal documents.

Visit Resources.AgingOptions.com

AGINGOPTIONS *LifePlanning*™

Family Planning

For Your Retirement

Aging Is a Family Affair

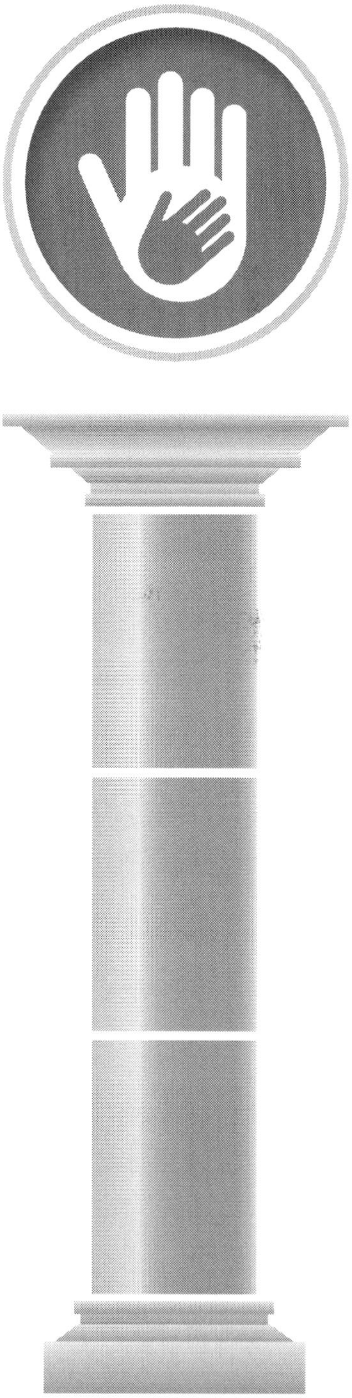

As we become older and move further into retirement, the saying "aging is a family affair" starts to become more poignant and closer to home.

Becoming a burden on family and loved ones is something no one wants. But when you reach the stage that you are no longer independent, no longer capable of handling your own affairs, your family and loved ones are pulled into your situation. They may be very willing to help you, as they feel it is the right thing to do. But what will be their experience...and yours? The question centers around how much planning you did, and how much instruction you gave your loved ones ahead of time. The burden you place on them is solely dependent on the planning you've done beforehand.

All the effort and thought you put into crafting legal documents, organizing your financial resources, your home's capabilities, and so on... will ultimately be a plan carried out by someone else. And unless that someone else is aware of your plans, and what is expected of them, and they are given an opportunity to have their input in the parts that impact them, you cannot be sure whether the plan you have pulled together will keep you from ending up in institutional care or becoming a burden on your named agents.

That is why a Family Meeting is so critical. However you define family, your fiduciaries are the ones who will make decisions on your behalf, and if you want them to feel less burdened—and for your wishes to come true in the process—they'll need to understand what it is you want in those circumstances, accept their responsibility, and have input in the planning process.

The point of having this Family Meeting is to clearly communicate your wishes to your named agents and family members.

By having an open discussion about your wishes and the roles your agents will have to play, everyone will know what is expected of them if and when a crisis comes to life.

Being transparent with your wishes will also help to minimize the burden you put on your loved ones; as well as ensuring that your wishes will be carried out the way you have planned. It will also minimize the chances of family feuds after you become incapacitated or die.

This too is the time where everyone hears each other's thoughts and commitments.

Since in the meeting you will share your plans and the roles you have assigned people, you will likely be given a lot of input, which may prompt you to make adjustments to the plan you initially prepared. Plus, it is valuable to know if someone feels that they are unable to meet your expectations.

LifePlanning Review

Before you can have an effective Family Meeting, you will need to clarify in your own mind what your plans are. Mapping out a clear blueprint from the other four pillars: Health, Housing, Financial, and Legal, should be done first. How will you provide Manuals of Instruction if you yourself don't yet know what you want them to do?

If you haven't already, this is a good time to transfer your Pause to Plan answers from the various sections of this book to the Blueprint section at the end. This will help you to consolidate your information into an easy-to-reference section for use when working with Professionals and for presenting during your Family Meeting.

Make sure you fill out the "**What It Means to Be Me**" form for you and your spouse (if married). This form can be found on page 194.

Let's recap your LifePlanning journey up to this point.

First, you created your **Health Plan**, since your health is your greatest asset. Better health reduces the chance that you'll face a housing or financial crisis, so this is your first—and ongoing —plan of action.

You learned the importance of a preventative health approach by setting goals for healthy habits.

Then, you learned about the Healthcare system and how to assemble the right team. We explored the two paths for Healthcare:

- **Using the insurance system**
- **Private Pay**

You should have selected a clinic, geriatrician, or other healthcare options that will help you avoid getting sick and maintain or improve your health.

Second, you worked on your **Housing Plan**. This is your most important, and often most difficult, decision throughout this process. It is crucial because a solid housing plan provides the predictability of outcome for your long-term goals. The theme of this part of your plan is to carefully define and select your forever home while you have plenty of independent retirement years ahead of you.

In housing, we updated the definition of home to mean the place where you can live out the rest of your life without needing to spend your final days in a nursing home or rehab facility. This should be the home you live in with enough time for it to become familiar. Additionally, your home selection process will take one of two paths:

- **Private Residence**
- **Retirement community**

Third, you prepared your **Financial Plan**. Ultimately, it's not just about how much money you have, but how you use it. The next steps for this phase of your *LifePlan* are to work with a Financial Planner and develop a thorough Financial Dashboard, as well as outline and assemble the team of professionals you trust.

As part of your Dashboard, you should have made choices for how to deal with Long-Term Care costs by choosing one or more of the following:

- **Private Pay**
- **Long-Term Care Insurance**
- **Public Assistance**

You understand that you'll need to make decisions at least five years in advance to protect your assets should you choose to apply for Medicaid or VA benefits.

Fourth, you mapped out your **Legal Plan**, highlighting preferences to discuss with your attorney.

You learned ways that you can:

- **Protect your assets** through the use of Wills and Trusts
- **Minimize burdens** on your loved ones through the use of legal documents

These documents protect your overall plan—what you put into these documents dictates how your wishes will be carried out. As your various trusts, powers of attorney, and other documents are drafted, the key is to insist that they read like a manual of instructions for your fiduciaries.

So, how are you doing in the *LifePlanning* process so far? Are you ready to proceed?

Family: Review *LifePlanning* Journey

After a review of the *LifePlanning* process: (Select one)

☐ I am ready to proceed

☐ I still have work to do, I'll come back later

Notes regarding my current *LifePlanning* status:

Family Meeting

Once you have completed the other sections, it is time to prepare a Family Meeting. In this meeting you will present them with the decisions you have made and explain your expectations, their roles and the resources that are available to them for your care. This is an exciting culmination of all your diligent effort regarding your retirement plans.

Let's break this down into two sections:

- **Planning Your Family Meeting**
- **During Your Family Meeting**

Planning Your Family Meeting

Planning a Family Meeting sounds easy, but to go in unprepared may waste not only your time and your family's time as well, but potentially create future hiccups in your planning. So, prior to your meeting, answer the following questions:

1. **When should you hold your Family Meeting?**
2. **What should you bring to the meeting?**
3. **Who should be invited?**
4. **Who should lead the meeting?**
5. **What issues should be discussed?**

Let's explore each question:

1) When should you hold your Family Meeting?

You should hold your Family Meeting only after you have made your decisions in the other sections of this book as we noted. Ideally, before the meeting you will have made your decisions in regards to:

- ☐ Your housing
- ☐ How you intend to fund care costs when the necessity arrives
- ☐ Your legal affairs
- ☐ Naming your fiduciaries and providing roles and resources to those you name

After you have reached those decisions, congratulations! It means you're ready to schedule the Family Meeting. As you complete the next steps of preparation, aim for scheduling the Family Meeting at a time and place convenient for your loved ones and conducive to an open discussion.

2) What should you bring to the Family Meeting?

Have a checklist for your Family Meeting and the decisions that you've recorded in each section of this workbook. For convenience, you can copy these decisions to the Blueprint section of this workbook. Also, be sure to bring copies of your "What It Means to Be Me" worksheet, as well as the relevant legal documents such as Powers of Attorney, Mental Health Advance Directive, and so on.

NOTE: We do not recommend giving a copy of your Will to heirs, on the chance that you decide to change your Will in the future.

3) Who should attend?

Although every circumstance is unique, we generally recommend including the following people in your Family Meeting:

- Anyone named as a Fiduciary
- Anyone named as a Beneficiary
- Spouses

First and foremost, you should include anyone named as one of your fiduciaries. It is also helpful to invite anyone you've declared as a beneficiary. Additionally, while it may be a decision that requires more consideration, depending on your personal situation we also recommend inviting the spouses of your fiduciaries. You may not be comfortable with some of the spouses of your fiduciaries, which also requires forethought before they are invited. However, if you decide to invite one spouse, you should invite them all. Alternatively, if you decide to leave out one of the spouses, you should not invite any. By doing this, you are helping to mitigate any drama, arguments, or negative feelings.

We recommend holding the meeting in person as opposed to virtually, if possible. There are two reasons for this. The first is that it can serve as a good indicator of who is or is not dedicated to the position as fiduciary. If one of your fiduciaries is too busy to attend, it may be a good idea to evaluate whether or not that person should remain a fiduciary. The second is that it is easier to gauge your family's reactions, both verbally and physically.

4) Who should lead the meeting?

We strongly suggest that a confident, neutral, and experienced third party lead the meeting. The reason is that in our experience, the moment you say you want them to ensure that you do not end up in a nursing home, they will more than likely become defensive. Shocked and offended that you would even consider that they would do anything to the contrary, they will begin to tune you out and the meeting will be pointless. By having a neutral third party lead the meeting, your family will likely listen to the same information and internalize it differently.

5) What should you discuss in the meeting?

We suggest that you be fully transparent with your family and loved ones during the meeting, letting them know your wishes, their roles, and what is expected of them. By communicating with clarity, you help to ensure that there is no confusion about your wishes and their roles when the time comes that you are no longer able to handle your own affairs. It also helps to mitigate any possible feuds.

There is a good chance that you will experience potential push-back from family members who feel they know what is best for you, regardless of your decisions. Make sure that you are prepared for this conversation, and you have all the details necessary to stave off criticism.

Although we recommend full clarity, we do suggest that you withhold details about your financial reality. By withholding this information, you do not provide your family with expectations of inheritance, which could possibly alter their decision-making as well as your relationship.

Use this page to make any additional notes regarding your Family Meeting.

Family: Planning Your Meeting

I have made the following decisions regarding my Family Meeting:

☐ When to hold my Family Meeting: (Date) ______________________________

☐ What I should bring: (List items)

____

____

☐ Who should be invited: (List)

____

____

____

☐ Who should lead: (Name) ______________________________

☐ What issues will be discussed: (List items)

____

____

____

Additional notes regarding planning my Family Meeting:

____

____

During Your Family Meeting

At the Family Meeting, have your Family Meeting Checklist in front of you along with your documents. Your moderator should also have a copy of your checklist to guide the meeting.

While there is no definitive outline of what should be discussed in sequence at a Family Meeting, we can provide you with some suggestions. Let's take a look.

Share Your Plans

First of all, this is the time to share your plans—including your long-term goals and objectives. You should outline your reasoning so that your loved ones can follow along and connect the dots between what decisions you are making now, what you'd like them to do, and why.

You should use this opportunity to provide your agents with copies of your Powers of Attorney, then read through them together, especially the parts that are regarding their duties and expectations.

For example, if you have written in a clause that instructs them to work with a specific Geriatric Care Manager and that they should do all they can to have you convalesce in your home, this is a great section to review carefully together.

Let each agent read his or her section out loud so everyone hears the same information in the same space. Then, ask them to interpret what they've read—having them paraphrase what they understood after reading. This helps to alleviate misunderstandings and confirms they know your expectations.

Continue with this method through any other documents and plans that you would like to share with them. Remember to discuss in detail any areas where they will eventually be executing your plan for you. It is important to hear that they understand your intent and wishes.

Review Your Resource Team

Be sure everyone knows of the individuals on your Professional Team. This list may be included as part of your legal documents or you can add it separately. The list includes service professionals such as Financial Planner, Tax Accountant, Property Manager, and so on. Your agents should know how to reach them and when they would need to connect with them.

Your Financial Power of Attorney will need to know where to access checkbooks, bank accounts, bills, etc. This may be a good time to talk through these details so others can be aware, too. Sharing the particulars of how each of the professionals from your list gets paid is important too, so there are no surprises.

This may also be a good opportunity to, at least generally, describe compensation that you've intended for those agents performing Power of Attorney, Trustee, or other responsibilities.

Listen and Get Input!

As you go through your plans, intents, and details together, a very important step is to solicit input and listen with an open mind. Remember that while you are aiming to minimize future burdens on them, your loved ones are processing this information in their own way, including the emotions of imagining future grief, along with pondering the logistics of what you expect of them. Their feedback may very well adjust parts of your plan. Housing plans are prone to adjustment after a Family Meeting. Be sure to review the Housing session, or any other where you may consider adjustments, following your meeting.

Promises and Making Commitments

After you have covered the issues you want to discuss, and before leaving the room, we highly recommend that you take the time to make promises to each other: you, to promise to listen to any concerns of your fiduciaries or loved ones and make amends in plans if necessary; and fiduciaries, to promise what they will or will not do in carrying out your designated plans. If these promises are made in earnest and are kept, then the rest is easier to navigate.

Family: During Your Meeting Checklist

During my Family Meeting, I did the following: (Select all that apply)

- ☐ Shared my plans
- ☐ Reviewed my resource team
- ☐ Listened and got input
- ☐ Made commitments

Notes from my Family Meeting:

After Your Family Meeting

Once you've completed your Family Meeting, it is important to follow up on the feedback you've received, and make any necessary changes.

Update Your Decisions

After your Family Meeting is concluded, check back in (around three months later) to make sure you and your named agents, as well as family members, are comfortable with the discussion, and inform them of any significant changes you've made. Ask for more feedback from them, if they haven't shared it already. Sometimes, having time to ponder brings up new thoughts, and it is good to hear them even if you don't ultimately make changes.

After your Family Meeting is concluded, contemplate your observations and the feedback you received from those who attended. Do you still feel confident in your choices of fiduciaries? Did anyone seem confused or concerned over the responsibilities you intend to place on them? Make any changes to your plans as necessary and be sure to update them in the applicable section of your *LifePlanning* Blueprint.

Follow up: Around three months later, check in on those who participated in your Family Meeting:

1. Make sure you and your named agents, as well as family members, are comfortable with things you discussed
2. Inform them of any significant changes you've made
3. Ask for more feedback from them, if they haven't shared it already

Sometimes, having time to ponder brings up new thoughts. Plus, it is good to inform them of any changes that you've made.

Update your Legal Documents

If you decide to make any changes to your fiduciaries, beneficiaries or other items listed in your legal documents, make sure to update these with your Attorney. Your documents are legally binding, so your changes need to be made official in your applicable documents.

Update Providers

You may realize at this point that you need to make adjustments to the professional resource team that you've selected. Maybe a family member has expressed concerns of a responsibility and you prefer to select a professional to handle the task. Whatever you choose, make sure you follow through by having the appropriate resource team.

If you ended up making any changes to legal or other documents, be sure to provide a final copy of them to all appropriate people, including your professional team, if applicable.

Implement Your *LifePlan*

With your *LifePlan* Decisions Blueprint completed, it is time to get to the work of implementing your plan. You should have new health goals to start on, a new medical team to find, financial and legal professionals to work with, and possibly new housing solutions to consider...

Let's get started!

It is important to remember that designing the *LifePlan* Blueprint was Phase 1, and completing the action steps from the Blueprint is Phase 2 – both phases are necessary to confidently say that you will AVOID:

1. **Institutional care**
2. **Becoming a burden on your family**
3. **Running out of money**

Once you've created your *LifePlan* Blueprint, now comes the work of implementing it. We recommend prioritizing each decision you have made and work on only one planning aspect at a time (Housing, Health, Financial or Legal) so that implementing the *LifePlan* does not become an overwhelming experience.

First Things First

Many of the steps in your *LifePlan* probably include working with a service professional, while other steps you will complete yourself. Deploying your *LifePlan* does not need to follow the same order of events as the creation of your Blueprint — you can implement your decisions in any order you choose.

Time Frame

The time it takes to implement a *LifePlan* is unique to each person. It depends on how quickly you find and schedule to meet with your professional resource team-members, make a housing decision, and find a time that is convenient for your family and loved ones to meet for a Family Meeting.

But from our experience, if you are diligent you will have completed your *LifePlan* after about six months. Remember to tackle one item at a time and be patient with yourself. Be sure to review your *LifePlan* regularly, about once a year, with your professional team or a *LifePlanner* Coach.

LifePlanning Blueprint

A *LifePlan* addresses the shortcomings of traditional planning by creating a comprehensive strategy that incorporates and coordinates the seemingly unconnected aspects of retirement planning, which then helps you anticipate and navigate whatever retirement issues arise. The premise is that proper planning anticipates the worst foreseeable scenarios and builds effective strategies to manage the circumstances.

Each section of this workbook contained worksheets designed to assist you in narrowing your preferences by providing various options. Your selections transform into a checklist of action items that you will need to implement in order to realize a comprehensive and coordinated *LifePlan*. After reading each segment and completing the applicable worksheets, carry your choices to this section. Once you have recorded all the action items into your Blueprint section, congratulations, you have your *LifePlan*!

So if you haven't done so already, start transferring your decisions from the worksheets into your *LifePlan* Blueprint.

Housing
Health
Private Residence
Develop Healthy Habits
Gather the Right Team

My Housing Plans

Housing: Requirements to Age in a Private Residence

I am interested in aging in a Private Residence:

- ☐ (**If yes**) My residence will meet the following requirements:
  - ☐ I will live in an Age-Friendly Home (the home and the location)
  - ☐ I have the Financial resources. (I can cover the cost of living at home and pay for care as needed.)
  - ☐ I have localized Family/Social support (Fiduciaries are within 5 miles and I will acquire a Geriatric Care Manager.)
- ☐ (**If no**) See Retirement Community Options

Notes regarding my ability to age in a Private Residence:

Housing: Private Residence Options

Select the options that reflect your preferences and make notes about what you would like to focus on regarding this topic.

My interest in Private Residence options:

- [ ] I am not considering a Private Residence
- [ ] I am interested in living in a Private Residence

The Private Residence housing options I'm considering are:

- [ ] N/A
- [ ] Remain in my current home
- [ ] Move to a new Age-Friendly home
- [ ] Move in with Loved Ones
- [ ] Move to a Lifestyle Community

Universal Design review for the home of my choosing: (if applicable)

- [ ] I plan to review the Universal Design for each home I'm considering

Notes regarding my Private Residence choice:

Housing: Retirement Community Options

My interest in Retirement Community options:

☐ I am not considering moving to a Retirement Community

☐ I am interested in moving to a Retirement Community

The Retirement Community options I'm considering are:

☐ N/A

☐ Independent Living

☐ Assisted Living

☐ Memory Care

☐ Residential Care Home (Adult Family Home)

☐ Skilled Nursing Facility

☐ Life Care Communities (CCRCs)

- ☐ I prefer a Type A - Extensive or Lifecare Contract
- ☐ I prefer a Type B - Modified Contract
- ☐ I prefer a Type C – Fee-for-Service Contract
- ☐ I prefer a Type D - Rental Agreement Contract
- ☐ I prefer a Type E - Equity Agreement Contract

☐ Undecided

Notes regarding my Retirement Community options: (Include areas of concern)

Notes:

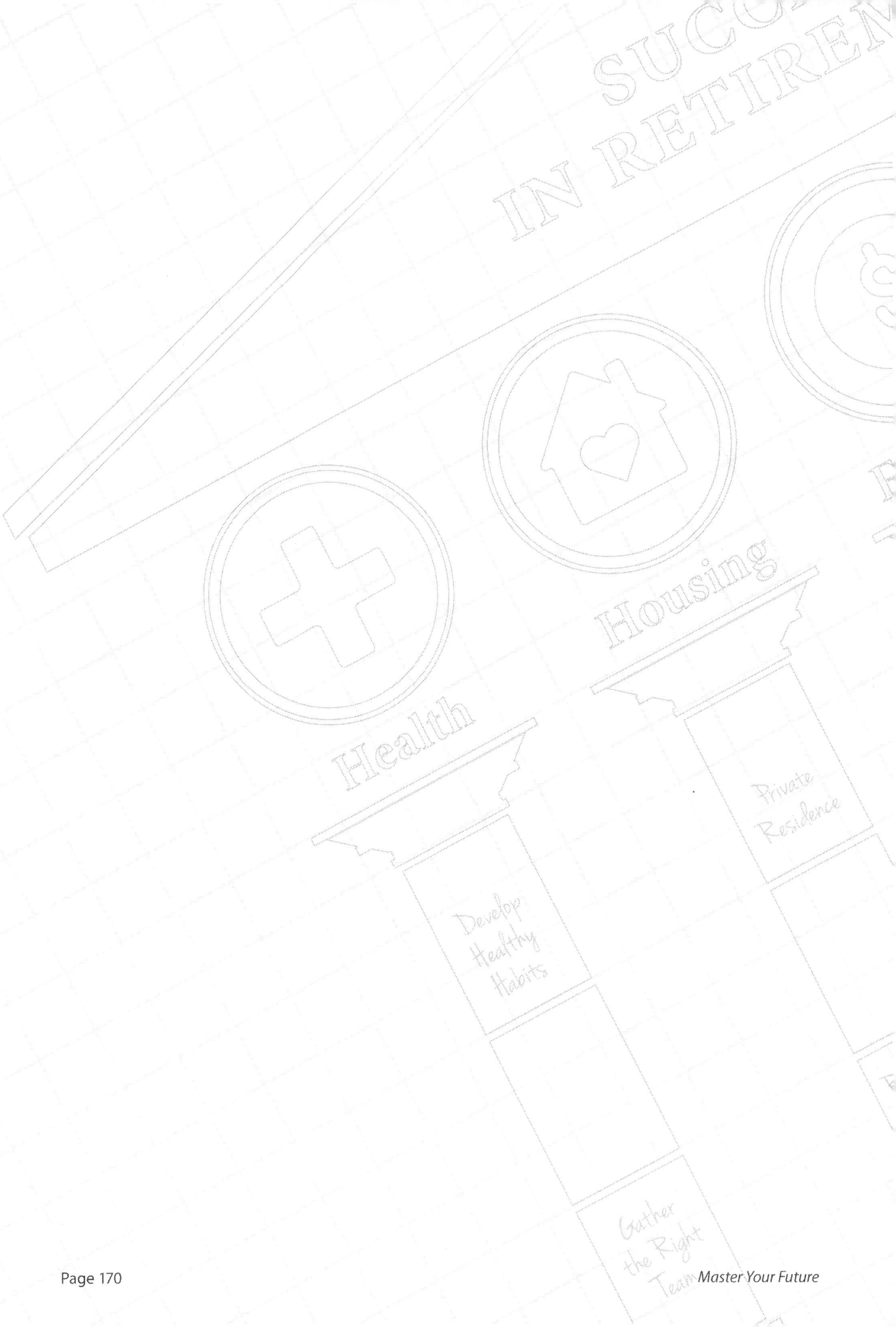
Health
Housing
Private Residence
Develop Healthy Habits
Gather the Right Team

My Health Plans

Healthy Lifestyle: Eat Right

My current eating habits are: (Select one)

- ☐ Excellent
- ☐ Fair
- ☐ Poor

I would like to meet with a nutritionist:

- ☐ Yes
- ☐ No
- ☐ Undecided

Notes regarding my Healthy Eating Plan:

Healthy Lifestyle: Exercise

My current physical activity level is: (Select one)

- ☐ Physically Fit
- ☐ Active
- ☐ Sedentary

My plan to improve my exercise includes: (Select all that apply)

- ☐ Joining a gym or other active group
- ☐ Checking if my insurance will cover gym memberships
- ☐ Monitoring my steps (via phone app or wearable device)
- ☐ Other

Notes regarding my exercise plan: (See goal suggestions)

Healthy Lifestyle: Socialize

My current meaningful social interactions are: (Select one)

- ☐ Frequent (daily meaningful interactions)
- ☐ Moderate (family and some social gatherings; somewhat superficial)
- ☐ Minimal (only essential interactions with others or with limited individuals)

My plan to increase meaningful social interactions includes: (Select all that apply)

- ☐ Volunteering in charitable/religious service
- ☐ Joining/engaging with hobby or civic groups
- ☐ Other

Notes regarding my Socialize Plan:

Health: Geriatricians

My plan to gather the right Geriatric Care Team: (Select all that apply)

- ☐ I already have a Geriatric Care solution
- ☐ I need to locate Geriatric options near me
  - ☐ Geriatric Care Clinics
  - ☐ Board-Certified Geriatricians
  - ☐ Physicians, PAs, or ARNPs with geriatrics training
  - ☐ Undecided

Notes regarding my Geriatric Care Plan:

Health: Private Pay Options

I plan to include the following Private Pay options in my Health team: (Select all that apply)

- ☐ Private/Preventative Care Clinics
- ☐ Concierge Care
- ☐ Wellness Science
- ☐ Undecided

Notes regarding my plan to include Private Pay options in my Health Team:

Notes:

Health
Housing
Private Residence
Develop Healthy Habits
Gather the Right Team

My Financial Plans

Financial: Dashboard Decisions

My Financial Dashboard Decision: (Select one)

- ☐ I am confident with my current Financial Plan
- ☐ I would like to create/review my Financial Plan

My Financial Dashboard will provide the following information: (Select all that apply)

- ☐ When is the ideal time to retire?
- ☐ When should I start Social Security benefits?
- ☐ How can I best maximize Social Security benefits?
- ☐ Should I invest in a long-term care insurance policy or not? If so, should it be a traditional policy, an asset-based policy, or a hybrid?
- ☐ Should I convert my traditional IRA accounts to Roth IRA accounts?
- ☐ How should I invest my assets?
- ☐ Other: (Note below)

My Financial Planner Decisions: (Select one)

- ☐ I have a Financial Planner that I like
- ☐ I would like to speak with a new Financial Planner
- ☐ I'm undecided

Notes regarding my Dashboard and Financial Planner:

Financial: Address Long-Term Care Costs

Answer this section after reviewing a thorough Financial Dashboard with your Financial Planner.

Long-Term Care: Private Pay Solutions

- ☐ I plan to utilize Private Pay for Long-Term Care
    - ☐ I will draw from my savings
    - ☐ I will use a reverse mortgage
    - ☐ I'm ready to speak with a Reverse Mortgage Specialist

Long-Term Care: Insurance Solutions

- ☐ I plan to use Long-Term Care Insurance
    - ☐ I will use a Traditional Plan
    - ☐ I will use an Asset-Based Plan
    - ☐ I'm ready to speak with a Long-Term Care Insurance Agent

Long-Term Care: Public Assistance Solutions

- ☐ I plan to use Public Assistance
    - ☐ I will apply for Medicaid
    - ☐ I will apply for VA Benefits
    - ☐ I'm ready to speak with an Elder Law Attorney for help qualifying for benefits

Notes regarding my plan to cover Long-Term Care Costs:

Financial: Minimize Burden on Others

I plan to minimize burdens on others by doing the following: (Select all that apply)

- ☐ Acquire a Financial Planner – and name them in my Agent Instructions with my Powers of Attorney
- ☐ Acquire an Accountant for Taxes – and name them in my Agent Instructions with my Powers of Attorney
- ☐ Set up Bill Pay – and detail my system for my Agents
- ☐ Set up Password Management – and make the list easily accessible to my Agents
- ☐ Prepay Final Expenses – and make the forms easily accessible to my Agents
- ☐ Acquire a Property Manager or Handyman – and name them in my Agent Instructions with my Powers of Attorney
- ☐ Arrange for a Geriatric Care Manager – and name them in my Agent Instructions with my Powers of Attorney.

Notes regarding my plan to minimize my burden on others:

Notes

Housing
Health
Private Residence
Develop Healthy Habits
Gather the Right Team

My Legal Plans

Legal: Protect Assets (Trust Protections)

I am interested in utilizing a Trust to protect my assets from the following threats:

(Select all that apply)

- ☐ Uncovered Long-Term Care Costs
- ☐ Subsequent Marriages
- ☐ Estate Taxes
- ☐ Inheritance risks

I would like to meet with an Elder Law Attorney to learn which trusts are best for me:

- ☐ Yes
- ☐ Not yet
- ☐ Undecided

Notes regarding my plan to protect my assets:

I plan to consult with my Attorney to align the following beneficiary designations:

(Select all that apply)

- ☐ Bank Accounts
- ☐ Brokerage Accounts (stocks, bonds, mutual funds, etc.)
- ☐ Retirement Accounts (IRA, 401(k), etc.)
- ☐ Life Insurance (annuities, etc.)
- ☐ Real Estate (houses, property, time shares, etc.)
- ☐ Business Ownership (Sole Proprietorship, LLC, Partnerships, etc.)
- ☐ Other

Legal: Minimize burdens

I plan to minimize burdens on others by acquiring the following: (Select all that apply)

- ☐ Healthcare Power of Attorney
- ☐ Financial Power of Attorney
- ☐ Mental Health Advance Directives
- ☐ Living Will (Advance Directives)
- ☐ Handling of Remains

I would like to meet with an Elder Law/Estate Planning Attorney to help me create my estate planning documents:

- ☐ Yes
- ☐ No
- ☐ Undecided

Notes regarding my plan to minimize burdens:

Legal: Choose Fiduciaries

When selecting fiduciaries: (Select all that apply)

☐ I plan to select family/loved ones as my fiduciaries

☐ I plan to select Professional fiduciaries

☐ I plan to name Co-Fiduciaries

Notes regarding my Fiduciary Plans:

Legal: Manuals of Instruction

I plan to include the following provisions for my Fiduciaries: (Select all that apply)

- [ ] Care Management
- [ ] Prohibitions
- [ ] Bar against Guardianship
- [ ] Professional Resources
- [ ] Compensation

Notes regarding my plan to create Manuals of Instruction:

Notes:

Housing
Health
Private Residence
Develop Healthy Habits
Gather the Right Team

What It Means to Be Me

SPOUSE 1

LifePlan: What It Means to Be Me ______________________

(Name of Spouse 1)

Entertainment for me means: (Select all that apply)

☐ **Reading**

The kinds of things I like to read include (fiction/nonfiction books, news, etc.):

The medium I prefer to read includes (books, magazines, newspapers, tablets, etc.):

☐ **Music**

The kinds of music I enjoy include:

Times when I like listening to music include:

Music I don't like includes:

☐ **Television**

The kinds of shows I enjoy include:

Time of day I enjoy watching includes:

☐ **Movies**

The kinds of movies I like to watch include:

Types of movies I don't like include:

SPOUSE
1 (Name)

Additional Entertainment Notes:

Pleasant surroundings for me means:

My Living Space preferences include (decorations, view, scents, etc.):

My Location preferences include (city vs rural, near water, near forests, etc.):

SPOUSE
1 (Name)

Healthy Habits for me means: (Select all that apply)

Eating Right

The foods I really enjoy eating include:

Foods I do not like include:

My food allergies or digestive challenges include:

Exercise / Activities

Places I enjoy visiting include:

Activities I enjoy include:

Socializing

The types of social interactions I enjoy include (large groups, close friends and family, religious visitors, etc.):

The frequency of social interactions I enjoy is (constant companionship, regular visits, or occasional check-ins):

SPOUSE
1 (Name)

Other things you should know about me:

My blood type is:

I have the following allergies:

I have the following chronic health conditions:

Additional notes about me:

SPOUSE

2 *LifePlan*: What It Means to Be Me ______________________

(Name of Spouse 2)

Entertainment for me means: (Select all that apply)

☐ **Reading**

The kinds of things I like to read include (fiction/nonfiction books, news, etc.):

The medium I prefer to read includes (books, magazines, newspapers, tablets, etc.):

☐ **Music**

The kinds of music I enjoy include:

Times when I like listening to music include:

Music I don't like includes:

☐ **Television**

The kinds of shows I enjoy include:

Time of day I enjoy watching includes:

☐ **Movies**

The kinds of movies I like to watch include:

Types of movies I don't like include:

SPOUSE
2 (Name)

Additional Entertainment Notes:

Pleasant surroundings for me means:

My Living Space preferences include (decorations, view, scents, etc.):

My Location preferences include (city vs rural, near water, near forests, etc.):

SPOUSE
2 (Name)

Healthy Habits for me means: (Select all that apply)

Eating Right

The foods I really enjoy eating include:

Foods I do not like include:

My food allergies or digestive challenges include:

Exercise / Activities

Places I enjoy visiting include:

Activities I enjoy include:

Socializing

The types of social interactions I enjoy include (large groups, close friends and family, religious visitors, etc.):

The frequency of social interactions I enjoy is (constant companionship, regular visits, or occasional check-ins):

SPOUSE

2 (Name)

Other things you should know about me:

My blood type is:

I have the following allergies:

I have the following chronic health conditions:

Additional notes about me:

Finished with Your Life Plan?

Now Organize it with the ***LifePlan* Organizer**: Mission Control for Your Life

If you've completed your *LifePlan*, **well done!** You've laid the groundwork for successful retirement, one where you avoid institutional care, avoid becoming a burden on loved ones, and have money left at the end.

Keep the benefits going by uploading your work to the

***LifePlan* Organizer!**

It's the nation's most powerful on-line platform for managing, sharing, and maintaining important information about your life, including detailed instructions for the people who will need them if you become injured, come down with an illness, or pass away.

Take advantage of everything ***The Portal*** has to offer!

You can access ***The Portal***, containing the *LifePlan* Organizer at:

Resources.AgingOptions.com

You can do this!

Thank you for letting us help you throughout this meaningful journey.

Confidence and peace of mind are yours — as you put protection and planning into action… accomplishing YOUR *LifePlan*.

We wish you well.

From all of us at AgingOptions, Age On!

Made in the USA
Coppell, TX
10 November 2026

11835567R00114